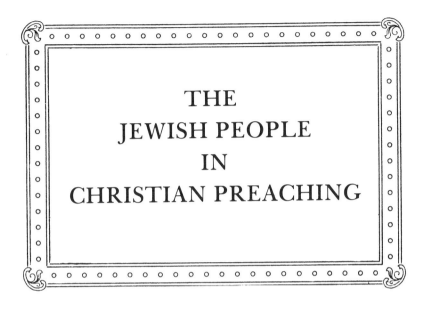

THE
JEWISH PEOPLE
IN
CHRISTIAN PREACHING

Edited by

Darrell J. Fasching

Symposium Series
Volume 10

The Edwin Mellen Press
New York and Toronto

Library of Congress Cataloging in Publication Data
Main entry under title:

The Jewish people in Christian preaching.

Papers based on a symposium "New horizons or old dilemmas?:
Judaism in Christian theology and preaching" held at the Temple
Society of Concord in Syracuse, N. Y., Oct. 15, 1979, co-sponsored by
Hendricks Chapel and the B.G. Rudolph Lectures in Judaic studies of
Syracuse University and the Syracuse Area Interreligious Council.
   Includes bibliographies and index.
   1. Judaism (Christian theology)--Congresses.
2. Preaching--Congresses.   3. Christianity and other religions--
Judaism--Congresses.   4. Judaism--Relations--Christianity--
Congresses.   I. Fasching, Darrell J., 1942-
II. Syracuse University.   III. Syracuse Area Interreligious Council.
BT93.J48   1984   261.2'6   84-16607
ISBN 0-88946-702-1

Symposium Series
Series ISBN 0—88946-989-X

The Edwin Mellen Press
P.O. Box 450
Lewiston, New York 14092

Printed in the United States of America

IN

MEMORY OF

SAMUEL SANDMEL

1911-1979

Acknowledgments

I gratefully acknowledge the permission of the Journal of Ecumenical Studies to reprint "Judaism in Christian Theology" by Paul van Buren as it appeared in Volume 18, #1, Winter 1981, pp. 114-127. It appears herein under the title "The Jewish People in Christian Theology".

The permission of the National Institute for Campus Ministry Journal is also gratefully acknowledged for the reprinting of "The Church, the Synagogue and the Gospel" by Darrell Fasching, which appeared in Volume 5, #4, Fall 1980.

I would also like to thank Elvira Pinder and Jill Lones for their diligence, patience and good humor in the preparation of this manuscript and Susan Segal for her careful proofing of the text. Appreciation is also expressed to James F. Strange, Dean of the College of Arts and Letters, the University of South Florida and to William C. Tremmel, Chairman, Department of Religious Studies for providing the services necessary to the completion of this book.

PREFACE

This book is the result of a symposium "New Horizons or Old Dilemmas?: Judaism in Christian Theology and Preaching" held at the Temple Society of Concord in Syracuse N. Y. on October 15th 1979. The event was co-sponsored by Hendricks Chapel and the B. G. Rudolph 'Lectures in Judaic Studies of Syracuse University and the Syracuse Area Interreligious Council. A note of thanks goes to Rev. Dr. John H. McCombe, then Dean of Hendricks Chapel, Dr. A. Leland Jamison, Director of the B. G. Rudolph Lectures and Mrs. Dorothy Rose, Executive Director of the Syracuse Area Interreligious Council. Without their support the symposium and this book would never have been possible. A word of appreciation is also due Rabbi Theodore S. Levy and the congregation of Temple Society of Concord for generously making their Temple facilities available for the Symposium. Finally a special thanks is due to Alan Berger, Assistant Professor of Religion and chairman of the Jewish Studies Program at Syracuse University. His constant interest, encouragement and aid allowed me to believe that the symposium and this book were realizable goals.

The immediate purpose of the symposium was to update clergy, religious educators and interested lay persons on recent developments in Christian theology relating to Judaism. Persons in these categories were invited from throughout upstate New York with the hope that the program would be of help to them in teaching and preaching in a way that would relate a positive attitude and appreciation of Judaism. We hoped as well that this event would be a positive sign to the Jewish communities in the area, indicating to them that something quite concrete was being done to overcome the past anti-judaic bias of the Christian tradition. Finally we had hopes, which the publicaton of this volume fulfills, that these goals might reach a larger audience.

The structure of the symposium is reflected in the first two parts of this volume. The morning was devoted to a consideration of "Judaism in Christian Theology" and the afternoon to "Judaism in Christian Preaching." We succeeded in engaging four of the most prominent scholars in the area of Jewish-Christian relations: Dr. Samuel Sandmel and Dr. Paul van Buren to address "Judaism in Christian Theology" and Dr. Eugene Fisher and Dr. Krister Stendahl to address "Judaism in Christian Preaching." Unfortunately Dr. Sandmel's serious

illness necessitated his withdrawal. In his place he recom-
mended his former student, friend, and colleague Dr. Michael
Cook who graciously accepted our invitation on rather short
notice. Not long after the symposium was held Dr. Sandmel
died. All of us who are involved in scholarship and dialogue
on Jewish-Christian Relations deeply grieve his passing. Our
lives shall not be the same without him, but his legacy in
scholarship and personal example is a rich one which we shall
all carry with us into the future. This book is dedicated to
Samuel Sandmel, in whose debt we all stand.

We sincerely hope that this volume effectively carries on
the commitment that so distinctively characterized Samuel
Sandmel's life; a commitment to enriching, deepening and
broadening the horizons of Jewish-Christian relations.

Darrell J. Fasching
Tampa, Florida
April 13, 1983

TABLE OF CONTENTS

Acknowledgments   iv

Preface   v

Introduction   ix

I

THE JEWISH PEOPLE IN CHRISTIAN THEOLOGY   1

Chapter One   The Jewish People in Christian Theology:
                 Past and Present
                     By Michael J. Cook   3

Chapter Two   The Jewish People in Christian Theology:
                 Present and Future
                     By Paul M. van Buren   19

II

THE JEWISH PEOPLE IN CHRISTIAN PREACHING   35

Chapter Three   The Jewish People in Christian Preaching:
                 A Catholic Perspective
                     By Eugene Fisher   37

Chapter Four   The Jewish People in Christian Preaching:
                 A Protestant Perspective
                     By Krister Stendahl   61

III

THE JEWISH PEOPLE IN CHRISTIAN PREACHING:
                 A HOMILY   77

Chapter Five   The Church, the Synagogue and the Gospel
                     By Darrell J. Fasching   79

IV

JEWISH-CHRISTIAN RELATIONS: PRESENT
          REALITIES AND FUTURE PROSPECTS 87

Chapter Six   Jews, Christians and the Future: What
                May We Hope For?
                     By Samuel Sandmel 89

Bibliography 105

Index 107

Scripture Index 110

Contributors 111

Introduction

Christianity stands in a unique relationship to Judaism; that of child to parent. The New Testament reflects the historical occurrence of the separation of the early Christian movement from its original Jewishness.

Though Christianity has been a separate religious tradition for centuries now, it still remains true that the very use of the New Testament in theology and preaching necessitates communicating some kind of image and understanding of Judaism. In this sense its use requires a discussion of Judaism in the preaching and teaching of Christian faith in a way that Jewish scriptures do not require a discussion of Christianity.

In the past, the way in which Judaism has been understood in Christian theology and preaching has all too often been negative and stereotypical. The consequences in terms of the history of the Christian treatment of Jews and Judaism have been tragic. But "one generation after" the Holocaust dramatic new developments have begun to take place. Christian theologians are now attempting to recover a more accurate and positive understanding of Judaism and of the relation of Christianity to Judaism.

There is clearly a new horizon of possibilities for a new age in Jewish-Christian relations. It is hoped that this volume will contribute to the dissolution of old dilemmas and to the expansion of this new horizon.

If there is a dramatically clear lesson to be learned from the history of Christian treatment of Jews, it is that words have the power to kill. Words are the bearers of images which shape attitudes and guide human action. When Jews are considered "legalistic", "stiffnecked" and "faithless" simply because they wish to preserve their traditions and remain Jews, imagery has been degraded into stereotype. When the early Church Fathers filled out this stereotype with accusations of deicide and used extreme vitriolic language, such as that of a John Chrysostom who on occasion described Jews as animals fit for slaughter, then hatred and death are in the air. It is a short step from such negative imagery to synagogue burnings and pogroms.

Whether in its classical Christian form or in its secular form, the attitude of the gentile has been one of refusal to allow the Jew to define his or her own identity and existence. The roots of this refusal have been traced, by some, directly to the New Testament and the doctrine of "supercession" that can be found there. This can be simply defined as the belief that Christians have replaced Jews as God's chosen people, therefore they are the true Jews. It follows that Jews really have no right to continue existing. This is "spiritual genocide"--the act of defining a people out of existence by appropriating their spiritual identity for one's own. It is this act which sets the stage and creates the precedents for the secular pseudo-religious program of physical genocide against the Jews by the Nazis. Words do indeed have the power to kill.

Words, in some sense, define reality--what is possible and what is necessary. In so far as Christianity defined being a Jew as a religious status, the "final solution" to the "Jewish problem" remained, at least officially, conversion and baptism, though the more ominous possibilities kept emerging in the eruption of pogroms and expulsions. Moreover the Jewish convert was never really trusted. Even with seculari- zation those Jews who may have wanted to assimilate found themselves damned if they did and damned if they didn't. Secularization, which seemed to promise the Jew equality with the gentile, brought only the equality of the great equalizer- death (in the Nazi concentration camps). If words define reality, and the secular redefinition of a Jew was racial, then the ancient stereotypes that continued to haunt the gen- tile psyche could only result in a new understanding of the "final solution" to the "Jewish problem". If being a Jew is a racial rather than a religious condition then conversion is no longer a "solution". The only logical "solution" is "genocide". Words do indeed have the power to kill.

But if words have the power to kill, the opposite should be equally true, words have the power to give life. Certainly this should be an implication of authentic "conversion" (i.e., change of heart) as it is understood in the Christian tradi- tion. If the unconverted or unrepentant heart spews forth words of death, then one true sign of repentance and conver- sion should be a change of language. If as Christians we say that we have been converted from death to life, then we ought to be prepared to recognize and root out the language of death wherever it still reigns in our hearts and psyches.

It is useful to remember that even where the apostolic writings exhibit the greatest hostility toward Judaism we are witnessing an argument between factions within a religious community. We have Jews arguing with Jews about what is the true observance of Judaism. The influx of gentiles into the Jewish sectarian movement which became Christianity, due to the relaxing of circumcision and other requirements of the Mosaic law for gentiles, rapidly changed the situation. All

too soon it was a gentile community that had taken over the
arguments of this once family disagreement. That shift in
context changed the meaning and import of the very same words.
The polar tension of disagreement about a shared identity
gives way to a dualism of insiders and outsiders; of gentiles
claiming to take the place of Jews in God's "plan".

It is coming to be recognized however, that the New
Testament writings themselves may offer other options than
that of supercession and spiritual genocide. There is in fact
more than one way for Christians to tell their story. As the
1975 statement of the U.S. National Conference of Catholic
Bishops put it: "In effect, we find in the Epistle to the
Romans (9-11) long neglected passages which help us construct
a new and positive attitude toward the Jewish people. There
is here a task incumbent on theologians, as yet hardly begun,
to explore the continuing relationship of the Jewish people
with God and their spiritual bonds with the New Covenant and
the fulfillment of God's plan for both Church and
Synagogue."[1] Instead of the old story of one covenant being
invalidated and replaced by another, it is suggested that a
two covenant story, in which each stands in a positive relation to the other, might be told.

The task "hardly begun" a few years ago is now under way.
The contributors to this volume are making important contribu-
tions to this task. There has been a great deal of literature
reflecting on the unfortunate and tragic past of Christian-
Jewish relations. The present volume is intended as a contribution to building a new and more positive future. It is
hoped that this will be a practical and useful book for the
preacher, the religious educator and the interested lay person. The objective is to help Christians tell their story in
a new way. We are talking about changing from a language of
death to one which gives life. We are talking about changing
imagery, attitudes and ultimately behavior.

In the process it is hoped that the Jewish community will
find the serious assumption of this task by Christians a
genuine cause for hoping that a truly new age is dawning in
Jewish-Christian relations. We realize of course that such
hopes have been dashed before and that the Jewish community
has every right to a healthy skepticism. We are talking of a
commitment then, on the part of Christians, that will have to
span generations in order to prove itself. Such commitments
can only be embraced by people of faith. Today, it is the
faith of Christians that is being tested to see if we are
really prepared to embody a conversion from death to life in
our lives.

The contributors to this volume address the question of
whether it is really possible for the Christian story to be

proclaimed in a new way in its teaching and preaching; and if so, just how that story might be told. The responses are contained in six chapters, organized into four parts--Part I: on "The Jewish People in Christian Theology," Part II: on "The Jewish People in Christian Preaching", Part III: on "The Jewish People in Christian Preaching - A Homily", and Part IV: "On Jewish-Christian Relations."

In chapter one, Dr. Michael Cook presents an assessment of "The Jewish People in Christian Theology: Past and Present" from a Jewish perspective. This chapter focuses on the development of the story of supercession in the apostolic writings and the Church fathers, noting the specific kinds of arguments that were advanced and the way in which the Rabbis responded to these new interpretations of the meaning of Judaism. Dr. Cook concludes with an assessment of the present situation in Jewish-Christian relations, noting both the difficulties and possibilities.

In chapter two, Dr. Paul van Buren speaks to the issue of "The Jewish People in Christian Theology: Present and Future." He explores the causes for the recent and dramatic change in Christian attitudes toward Jews and Judaism. He then goes on to suggest the future shape of a Christian theology which takes seriously the existence of the Jews as God's first and ongoing covenant people. Dr. van Buren explores the significance of an on-going two-covenant theology for Christians in relation to their understanding of the Church, God as Trinity, Christ, Revelation and the Bible.

With chapter three, we enter the second part of this volume which addresses the question of Christian preaching. Here Dr. Eugene Fisher reflects on "The Jewish People in Christian Preaching: A Catholic Perspective." He reviews the considerable success he believes Christians have had in rooting out negative stereotypes of Judaism from their teaching and preaching. He then goes on to consider the more difficult problem of defining the positive relation between the two covenant communities. Here he focuses upon the central Christian "promise-fulfillment" theme as it relates the two testaments and the two covenant communities in Christian theology and preaching.

In chapter four Dr. Krister Stendahl offers some thoughts on "The Jewish People in Christian Preaching: A Protestant Perspective." He reminds the preacher that in Luther's view, the word of God is not simply the word in the Bible. In some sense it only becomes the word of God when preached. He suggests that the preacher is not only responsible for what is said but what he or she is heard or understood to have said. Dr. Stendahl concludes by suggesting a number of ways of communicating the gospel so as to witness to the "good news" without having to tell "nasty stories" about one's Jewish neighbor.

Part three is made up of a single sermon, a homily on the theme of "The Jewish People in Christian Preaching," which was originally offered by Darrell Fasching at Hendricks Memorial Chapel, Syracuse University, in conjunction with the Symposium on which this book is based. This sermon received a National Institute for Campus Ministry Sermon Award, appearing in the Fall 1980 issue of the NICM Journal. Here Dr. Fasching recalls the tragic history of the church's use of sterotypes of the Jewish People derived from John's Gospel, with its theme of the "blindness of the Jews". He argues that John must be interpreted in the light of Paul and Isaiah, in which the gentile-Christian covenant receives its holiness and legitimacy by being grafted into the covenant of th Jewish People, who express their covenant in a "blindness of faith," trusting not in their own sight, but rather in God to lead the way.

Chapter six provides the content for the fourth and con- cluding part of this volume. Here we have reflections on "Jew, Christians and the Future: What May We Hope For?" by the man to whom this volume is dedicated-- Samuel Sandmel.

Dr. Sandmel's death deeply grieved all of us who have any concern for Jewish-Christian relations. His scholarship and his personal commitment have left us a rich legacy. This final chapter brings together selections from his book WE JEWS AND YOU CHRISTIANS, originally published by J. B. Lippincott Company and now out of print. We are grateful to Mrs. Frances Fox Sandmel for her gracious permission to reprint this material. These selections provide a forthright and helpful comparison of the differences and similarities between Jews and Christians, and an honest appraisal of what might be legitimately hoped for in the area of Jewish- Christian relations. Dr. Sandmel's candor and compassion provide a fitting conclusion to this volume which owes so much to his scholarship and his spirit.

---

[1]Stepping Stones to Further Jewish-Christian Relations, p. 33. This is an unabridged collection of Christian documents, compiled by Helga Croner (London & New York: Stimulus Books, 1977). It is available from the Anti- Defamation League of B'nai B'rith, 823 United Nations Plaza, New York, N.Y. 10017. This volume contains the major statements on Judaism by Protestant and Catholic church bodies in the United States, Latin America and Europe. It is an excellent source and a copy belongs in every church and synagogue library.

PART ONE:

THE JEWISH PEOPLE IN CHRISTIAN THEOLOGY

CHAPTER ONE

THE JEWISH PEOPLE IN CHRISTIAN THEOLOGY: PAST AND PRESENT

Michael J. Cook

In reflecting on the theme of "Judaism in Christian Theology," I shall first review the trends of the past, then shift my focus to the modern situation, with an eye to the future.

I

I wish I could tell you that, on the subject at hand, I speak for all Jews - that is, that what I bring you is a clearly articulated Jewish reaction to the topic of "Judaism in Christian Theology". Yet the fact remains: we Jews have no creeds, central synods or chief spokespersons vested with the authority to make pronouncements on our behalf; accordingly, we have no official positions which I can simply appropriate and pass on for your attention.

Moreover, even if I could summon up such official pronouncements, it is possible that none would address the subject: "Judaism in Christian Theology." The reality of the situation is the following: since the Christian religion was born within the Jewish, in your history you have faced the need to define your relationship toward Jews in a way in which we have not felt the need to do toward you. The great likelihood is that, even were Jews in the habit of producing clearly defined stances on many facets of our religious existence, we would have no occasion to address in an official manner the particular subject at hand. In limiting my remarks, therefore, to what are only personal observations and reactions, I shall begin by sharing with you my most vivid impressions concerning earliest Christian theology in relation to Jews and Judaism.

II

While Jews of old believed that they lived in a covenant with God, and were the special and permanent objects or recipients of his chosenness, the early Christians came to believe

- and wished to justify their belief - that they had supplanted the Jews in God's favor, that they had become the "New Israel." Moreover, while Jews believed that the Bible was already complete, the early Christians wished to persuade others that Christian theological beliefs were not only a continuation of the Jewish Bible beyond the termination point assumed by the Jews, but were indeed underpinned and justified by Jewish Scriptual texts. Still further, while Jews in early Christian times felt that the existence or non-existence of Christianity had no bearing on the excellence of Judaism, Christians came to feel that, for Christianity to assert its supremacy, Judaism had to be shown as being possessed of less value - and whatever value it was accorded had to be construed as a function of God's plan in preparing the way for Christianity.

In carving out its own identity through the process of dialectic with the mother religion, Christianity came to dissect Judaism into three components. The first component consisted of those elements of Judaism which Christianity appropriated virtually in their entirety and without significant alteration; as the most notable example, we can think of the Jewish Scriptures, albeit in Greek translation. The second component consisted of those elements of Judaism which Christianity would not simply adopt but also adopt through significant alteration, such as aspects of the Jewish calendar, patterns of Jewish worship, the synagogue structure, the use of bread and wine and indeed the very way in which the image of the Messiah came to be described and understood. The third component consisted of those elements of Judaism which Christianity eventually abandoned completely, such as the Jewish dietary laws and circumcision. Once thus dissected and stripped, Judaism was then to assume its status as a kind of carcass no longer needed and certainly no longer vibrant. Completing this process, developing Christianity added the many innovations unique to itself: new institutions, new officialdom, and new rituals and practices.

The end result has been a sad one indeed. We have witnessed here a process wherein religious divisiveness became sharp even between parties who shared most of their essentials in common. The limited areas of theological disagreement came to be the focus of special attention, and eventually emerged as the breeding ground for intense hostility, especially because the parties entered into competition with one another for the same adherents. Ultimately, whenever Christian theology mentioned Jews or Judaism, the avenues of such expression came almost always and almost necessarily to be avenues of denigration.

III

Central to this denigration of Judaism in emerging Christian theology is the early Christian assertion that God had made a "new covenant" with a "New Israel." The fulcrum of this assertion was held to be Jeremiah 31:31. Jews have long since been aware of what Jeremiah intended by this passage, and Jewish exegetes of old became alarmed at seeing the way its import was now undergoing revision.

Before the time of Jeremiah, Israelite history had been punctuated by prophetic utterances warning that God might nullify his covenant with Israel. Such were the predictions of Amos and Isaiah in particular. The fall of the Northern Kingdom in 722 B.C.E. had seemed a dramatic confirmation that God had indeed nullified his covenant with Israel, and the conquest of the Southern Kingdom in 597 only seemed to render that conclusion all the more assured.

Jeremiah addresses himself to this crisis. He notes that the evidence indicates that the covenant of old seems ruptured, but he then announces that all is not lost - indeed, there is still hope, for God would now establish a "new covenant," that is a perpetual and never-to-be-annulled covenant, defining and renewing God's continuing relationship with the Jewish people, and pledging that God and the Jewish people would continue in such a union forevermore.

Early Christian exegetes, however, co-opted Jeremiah's "new covenant," and applied it to their own community as the "New Israel". The Pharisees and rabbis of old had always believed that, when God had a revelation to communicate to the Jews, he would do so directly and unmistakably through entirely Jewish channels - and yet no Jewish writing ever hinted at a concept of a "New Israel" supplanting the Jews. If God had indeed cast off the Jews, why was it only Christian interpretations that so alleged. Clearly, such Christian interpretations were adjudged by Jewish exegetes erroneous.

IV

Within the arena of emerging Christian theology, the following question inevitably arises: If Christians have indeed supplanted Jews, then what shall we construe has happened to the Jews as a result of this act of supercession? Early Christian theology supplies us with a variety of responses ranging from that of Paul to those of some of the Church Fathers. In the final section of Paul's argument in Romans 9-11, Paul indicates that Israel's apostasy is not final, and neither is God's rejection of his people. In fact, the difficulty created by the seeming rejection of the Jews is largely resolved by the notion that their apostasy is only a necessary stage in an overarching process which will result in all people's knowledge of God's grace.

As a matter of fact, there is even now, Paul argues, a chosen remnant of Israel which has been selected by grace and hence not rejected. Yet as for others, a hardening has temporarily come over most of Israel so that, in the interim, the full number of the gentiles might have an opportunity to hear and embrace the gospel and thereby become saved. Israel as a whole will eventually be moved by intense jealousy at seeing her own possession now in the hands of the gentiles - indeed, her jealousy will be so intense as to induce her then to accept what she now rejects. Then it will be not simply a remnant but rather all Israel who will enter the Kingdom of God and be saved. Such are the ways of God's unfathomable wisdom that Israel's rejection by God will eventually become the very key to her salvation. Ironically enough, though Jews by and large have found the message of Paul to be unpalatable to them personally, they have clearly preferred Paul's attitude to the Jews as expressed in Romans to the attitude toward the Jews advanced by certain spokesmen for the later church. For Jews feel that later Christian theology itself came to ignore or, at the very least, to depart from a number of the positions advanced by Paul himself, in Romans in particular.

Paul, in Romans, rather lengthily defends the advantages the Jewish people themselves had in terms of being chosen, and he emphasizes that Israel's rejection by God is only temporary. Yet in the decades after Paul died, at least three factors conspired to redirect early Christian theology along lines Paul himself apparently never intended.

One factor was the unavoidable observation that Jewish resistance to Christianity showed no signs of abating; accordingly, it was becoming increasingly difficult to accept Paul's contention that some day the Jews would after all accept Jesus as the Christ. A second factor was the following: Paul himself had been a Jew, and thus there had been in his case at least a measure of positive personal orientation toward those who were his fellow Jews; but this was a positive kinship with Judaism which later Christian spokesmen did not and probably could not share.

A third and undeniably central factor in these later developments was the calamitous fall of Jerusalem and the destruction of the Temple in the year 70 C.E., events heralded throughout the Roman Empire as the triumph of Jupiter over the God of Israel, but serving Christianity in particular as an astounding confirmation of the rejection of the "Old Israel" and the replacement of the Jews by the "New Israel". While Paul considered the rejection of the Jews to be only temporary, and looked forward to their eventual salvation, the destruction of the Temple was an event so catastrophic in nature as to imply the permanence of the Jews' rejection and the intensity of God's wrath with his people.

What is instructive to note here is how all these developments led to a departure of developing Christian theology from the attitudes and interpretations advanced by Paul himself in his Epistle to the Romans. Whereas Paul had alleged that there existed a divine mystery whereby "all Israel will be saved" (Romans 11:26), and that the hardening which had come over the Jews was only temporary, certain Patristic writings came to present the Jews as the hopeless enemies of the church; their rejection was now deemed permanent and their chances of salvation nil. Whereas Paul asked the question in Romans, "Has then God rejected His people?" (Romans 11:1), with his answer being, "By no means!", the reply of certain later church spokesmen was, in effect, "By all means!" Whereas Paul in Romans has queried, "Then what advantage has the Jew?" (Romans 3:1), and then had proceeded to spell it out in an affirmative fashion, when the later church asked the question, "Then what advantage has the Jew?" its answer seems to have been, "None whatsoever."

Thus for example, the Epistle of Barnabas espouses the extreme position: though God had indeed extended the offer of Chosenness to the Jews, Israel had never really accepted the covenant of election in the first place. Immediately after the offer had been extended, Israel had taken to idol worship, building the Golden Calf, as a result of which God immediately suspended the proposed covenant which he had contemplated. God, we are told, thus never actually concluded the covenant with Israel; he decided to reserve it instead for the later Christians. This is surely a significant departure from the Pauline viewpoint in the Epistle to the Romans.

This kind of departure was carried one step further by Justin Martyr who, in his Dialogue with Trypho, contended that the whole purpose of God's making a covenant with Israel was not for Israel's benefit but rather for Israel's condemnation. Not only are the Law, circumcision, and the Sabbath no longer of any validity - they are actually evidence of God's rejection of Israel! Circumcision was a branding of the Jews, a punishment both for the slaying of Jesus and for "cursing in your synagogues those who believe on Christ."[1] "We too," Justin goes on to allege, "would serve the flesh circumcision, and the Sabbaths, and...all the feasts, if we did not know for what reason they were enjoined you, namely, on account of your transgressions and the hardness of your hearts."[2]

In sum, therefore, Paul's assertions to the effect that Israel's rejection was only temporary evolved into a conviction by others that she was never the elect and into the subsequent accusation that God's particular relationship to Israel was in essence to her disadvantage and damnation. Later Patristic writings, moreover, in some cases intensified the anti-Jewishness of their predecessors. A number of the most grotesque examples are furnished by the sermons of St. John Chrysostom, to the effect that "the synagogue...is not only a theatre, it is a place of prostitution,...a den of thieves and hiding-place of wild animals,... not simply of animals, but of impure beasts," and also to the effect that "The Jews in shamelessness and greed surpass even pigs and goats... The Jews are possessed by demons, they are handed over to impure spirits.... Instead of greeting them and addressing them as much as a word, you should turn away from them as from the pest and a plague of the human race."3

V

What was the Jewish response to these Christian theological themes? Jews of ancient times were probably caught off guard by the growth of Christianity, an unexpected development especially because of the persecution and martyrdom Christians had undergone. Undoubtably, Jewish concern was heightened when, ultimately, Rome adopted Christianity as its imperial religion, for now Christianity's animus against Judaism had become allied with the political arm of Roman officialdom.

From the Jewish theological perspective, among the most bewildering of developments was the way in which Jewish Scriptures had come to be appropriated and utilized in the interests of Christian ideology. The early rabbis, and the Pharisees before them, had prided themselves on their mastery of exegtical technique. Indeed, during the early Hasmonean times, in the second century B.C.E., when the Pharisees had first emerged to prominence they elicited popular respect through their expertise in fashioning and implementing new principles of Scriptual exegesis. By alleging that God had imparted to Moses a two-fold revelation, an oral as well as a written Torah, and by establishing for themselves a monopolistic mastery of the principles for interpreting this allegedly new revelation, the Pharisees had become well aware of how new insight into Scripture could become the handmaiden of ideological and theological as well as political revolution. Thus it is that the Pharisees and later the rabbis fully grasped the potentialities inhering in specifically Christian Scriptual exegesis.

They noted uneasily that Christian theology was enlisting three sources of authority: 1) the words of Jesus; 2) the words of Jewish Scripture; and 3) what Christians termed the Holy Spirit. The first two sources were mutually supportive: Jesus was believed himself to have quoted Jewish Scripture, and Jewish Scripture, in turn, was held to be predictive of

Jesus' coming. The third source, meanwhile, the Holy Spirit, firmly anchored the early Christians - who alleged that it was the Holy Spirit which furnished their exegetes with the insight to see the Scripture in an innovative way, that is, as reflective and predictive of the coming of Jesus.

Because gentiles were not as familiar with Jewish Scripture as were many Jews, the early Christians encountered fewer obstacles in convincing Gentiles that Jewish Scripture was the underpinning of Christian theological preachment. The Pharisees and the early rabbis, however, had an alternative notion about the meaning of Scripture. They lodged, as Jews of today still lodge, two objections in particular. First, they objected to the assumption by the early Christians that the Scripture was not in finished form in and of itself but rather was incomplete and predictive of something later in time. Second, they objected that Scripture was being interpreted by Christians in the light of whatever it was which Christians thought came later - and that, in the Jewish view, this produced a certain kind of distortion. Parts of Scripture which had not initially seemed so especially important now seemed to receive a disproportionate emphasis, while parts of Scripture which had long been interpreted one way now suddenly came to be interpreted in a quite different and, in the judgment of the rabbis, a quite erroneous fashion. In other words, Jews were unable to accept the Christian allegation that Jewish Scripture was a book about Jesus the Christ - for example, that in the Song of Songs the Christ was addressing the church, that there could be found in Isaiah's Suffering Servant descriptions of Jesus himself, or that in the crossing of the Red Sea one could discern God's deliverance of the Christian from bondage to sin.

Meanwhile, Jewish reactions to Pauline theology were likewise reactions of unease. To Jewish ears, Paul seemed to be saying the following: The fulfillment which Jews have throughout their history been seeking has actually already taken place, but the Jews have failed to recognize what they have waited so long to see. Blindness is itself unfortunate, but blindness to the fulfillment of one's own heritage is a tragedy beyond comprehension. The Jews were not chosen because of any merit; for election is not the result of anything we can do to deserve it. It was accorded the Jews only by the free choice of God. Yet what cannot be won by merit can indeed be forfeited by negligence, and not only can election be forfeited, but in the case of the Jews in particular, it has indeed already been forfeited. The Gentiles, who never pursued righteousness, have attained it, whereas the Jews, who have always pursued it, have missed it altogether. The Jews have all along misunderstood the meaning of righteousness - righteousness is the status which God confers on those who humbly receive it through faith as his gift, whereas Jews have foolishly assumed that righteousness is a kind of life we can succeed in attaining based on obedience to the Law. Clearly, it is reasonable to assume that Jews were not receptive to these sentiments, nor to the even more severe theology of the Church Fathers.

VI

When discussing the portrayal of Judaism in Christian theology, many Christians inquire: Is Christian anti-Jewish theology to be traced only as far back as the sermons and writings of the Church Fathers, or is anti-Jewishness rooted in the texts of the New Testament itself? Often the request is made of Jews not to have their view of the New Testament determined or even influenced by what later Christian preachers themselves have said. If New Testament texts have been misused and abused for purposes of marshalling anti-Jewish sentiment, it would be unwarranted to attribute to the New Testament itself the sentiments of writers post-dating it.

Five arguments have been commonly advanced by those who strenuously defend the New Testament from charges of anti-Jewishness:

First, since the New Testament is inspired by God, it cannot be antiJewish. The Gospel is the ultimate revelation of divine love; as such, it could in no way have been designed to encourage the contempt of any people or to contribute to the growth of misunderstanding or hatred in the world. Moreover, Jesus spoke the language of love, he preached the turning of the cheek and even the love of one's enemies. It would therefore be totally anomalous for those writing his teachings, and deeply committed to him themselves, to have written works which are anti-Jewish.

A second argument admits that there is harsh language directed against the Jews in certain sections of the New Testament, the gospels in particular, but avers that this is simply prophetic rebuke out of love. Even the Prophets had availed themselves of severe language in rebuking the Jewish people, and surely the Prophets are not to be adjudged anti-Jewish. Similarly, prophetic-like rebukes, as we often find them in the New Testament, are a kind of literary or oratorical style. Maledictions against the Jews - whether by Jesus or Paul or the Prophets of old - were not meant to be final but were merely devices intended to shock people into repentance before it was too late.

A third argument advanced is the following: the gospels distinctly show us that a part of the Jewish people opposed Jesus. Many passages indicate that the common people with whom he was so popular recognized him as their prophet. It was only the Jewish leaders, especially the chief priests and

the Pharisees, who were responsible for the opposition and
enmity which eventuated in the Crucifixion. These are the
ones portrayed in the New Testament as Jesus' enemies, not the
Jewish people as a whole.

A fourth argument emphasizes that Jesus valued Judaism,
and that Jesus and his disciples were Jews; so also was the
earliest church in Jerusalem Jewish in tenor. Many of Jesus'
teachings were specifically those of Judaism. How, then,
could writers of the New Testament possibly have been anti-
Jewish?

Fifth, and above all, it is argued that we should not
confuse the interpretations of later preachers on the New
Testament with the attitude of the New Testament itself.
While a number of the Church Fathers and Christian homileti-
cians were definately ill-disposed toward Jews and Judaism, we
should recognize that they read the New Testament in the light
of events which took place much later - they interpreted the
New Testament texts long after the New Testament was written,
at a time in the third and later centuries when Christian
preachers were forging new weapons for the church in her
ongoing conflict with Judaism. Interpreting the gospel, they
added their own errors and prejudices to the holy and eternal
and infallible truths of the New Testament itself. These were
interpretations of later preachers, however, and were not
inherent in the New Testament texts themselves.

In responding to these five arguments, many Jews aver
that the pejorative description of Judaism in later Christian
theology takes its cue directly from the New Testament itself.
For example, while not denying that Jesus and the early
Jewish-Christians, valued Judaism, Jews nevertheless
distinguish between the favorable attitude toward Judaism by
Jesus and early Jewish Christians, on the one hand, and the
negative attitude toward Judaism by the later gospel writers,
on the other. Jews believe that, quite possibly because of
Jewish resistance to Christianity in the years after Jesus'
death, the four Evangelists came to denigrate the very Judaism
which Jesus himself had valued.

As for the argument that we should not confuse the anti-
Jewish interpretations of preachers later than the New
Testament with the attitude of the gospel writers themselves
(that the preachers admittedly were, in some cases, anti-
Jewish, but the gospels themselves were not), Jews have
advanced the following response: just as later preachers may
have been investing their personal biases into their commentaries on the New Testament, so also may the four Evangelists
themselves have given vent to their personal ill-will toward
Jews in their very act of describing Jesus' life in their
gospels.

While Jews welcome the suggestion that the admittedly harsh language against the Jews in the gospels is simply prophetic rebuke out of love, at the same time there is the nagging feeling that the gospels' denunciations of the Jewish people far exceed any rebuke by the Prophets of old. In the Jewish perception, the Prophets were acting out of love for and loyalty to the Jewish people - the message of the Prophets is designed to solidify the bonds of God's covenant with the Jews. The rebukes in the New Testament, however, predict that God will choose another people to replace the Jews. While Jesus himself may have rebuked the Jewish people out of love, the particular intensity and animosity which characterize some of the denunciations attributed to him most likely reflect interjections of the Evangelists, not the sentiments of the historical Jesus himself, and these redactional elements are unavoidably to be construed as definitely anti-Jewish.

As for the argument that the New Testament, since it is inspired by God and constitutes the ultimate revelation of divine love, cannot be anti-Jewish, Jews do not wish to respond insensitively. At the same time, since Jews do not consider the New Testament to be divinely inspired, and therefore do not include the New Testament in their Bible, this argument is not seen as compelling by Jews.

The remaining argument, however, strikes a different chord - and this is that the gospels distinctly show us that only a part of the Jewish people opposed Jesus. A great many, indeed thousands according to the gospels themselves, became his followers. How then can the same gospels which show us thousands of Jews accepting his message, or at least eager to hear what he had to say, be considered by modern Jews as anti-Jewish?

A Jewish response pursues the following line. A different situation prevails today from what was the case in the first century. In the first century, a Jew could become a Christian and still remain a Jew. In this sense it is true that the gospels are not biased against all Jews, they are only biased against Jews who do not accept Jesus. They are not biased against Christian-Jews, but they are biased against non-Christian Jews.

Today, however, from the Jewish point of view, there can be no such person as a Jewish-Christian. After nineteen centuries of a parting of the ways, the theological distinctions between Jews and Christians are so formidable that no one can genuinely be both a Jew and a Christian. This is particularly the case because the conception of the Messiah in modern Christianity seems to Jews quite at variance with the image of the Messiah affirmed by the earliest Jewish-Christians. From the Jewish point of view, a Jew who today professes belief in Jesus as the Messiah is a Christian by definition and not a

Jew. In effect, then, the only persons mentioned in the gospels with whom Jews today can identify is with those Jews who do not accept Jesus, and the gospels are harsh on these people.

Jews do not ask that Christians agree that parts of the New Testament are anti-Jewish but only that Christians understand how Jews can see it that way, especially given the fact that many Christian preachers have not only used the New Testament in precisely that fashion but may have felt justified in doing so because they believed the anti-Jewishness of their sermons derived from the New Testament texts themselves.

VII

It is my feeling, and I am gratified to note, that Christian clergy are becoming increasingly aware of the sensitivities of Jews to the role in which Judaism has been cast in Christian theological formulations. Yet I am not convinced that prospects for the immediate future are especially sanguine.

To be sure, in the area of interfaith relations, many seemingly encouraging signs have been surfacing in recent years. Relations between rabbis and Christian clergy have, in many instances, become very warm and cordial, not only on the college campus and in the chaplaincy but on the community scene in general, where we witness the practice of interfaith Thanksgiving worship services and exchanges of pulpit assignments between Jewish and Christian preachers. I also note the extensiveness of interfaith cooperation in civil affairs, not to mention the promotion by Christian clergy and academicians of chairs in Jewish studies in American colleges and universities. Moreover, some efforts have been made, in producing Christian teaching materials, to edit out anti-Jewish references, and to present Judaism as having a valid basis of its own in terms of a convenantal relationship with God.

Nevertheless, of the old problems which still abide perhaps the most significant is the following: the average churchgoer usually remains untouched by whatever is accomplished on the level of their clergy in institutes such as this one. The spirit of camaraderie which often eventuates from the interfaith dialogue among Jewish and Christian clergy and academicians rarely filters down and becomes translated or implemented on the lay level. While Christian clergy learn more about Jews and Judaism through personal contact and through study, the average Christian churchgoer remains out of touch with these changing developments. For him or her, the most direct pipeline to Jews and Judaism remains the one provided by the Christian Scriptures which Christian churchgoers read and hear so frequently and which undoubtably and unavoidably contribute to anti-Jewish feeling.

History has taught the Jewish people that, when anti-Jewishness resulted in physical harm for the Jews, that harm was not inflicted directly by the church as an institution but rather directly from the Christian masses, influenced as they were by the effect of the church's scriptural interpretation on its indoctrinated faithful. It was the aroused Christian mob rather than the church itself that inflicted injury and death on the Jew. Accordingly, Jews do not pay as much attention to the Christian clergy as they do to the Christian laity, and the Christian laity read and understand Christian Scripture with less breadth of understanding than do their clergy.

Let me offer an analogy throughout Jewish history, the Jewish teachers have found a way of altering the spirit of Scripture even without necessarily producing changes in the text. The result is that Judaism is not dependent on Jewish Scripture as much as on emphases of Scripture as defined through the filter of rabbinic perceptions. The greatest authority in Judaism resides not in the Bible but in what the rabbis have said and continue to say that the Bible means. Hence, the rabbinic tradition not only may alter but even override Scripture.

From the Jewish and I believe the Christian perspectives, however, no comparable authority seems to reside in post-Biblical Christian compendia commenting verse by verse on New Testament Scripture, so that the average churchgoer is exposed to no authorized or authoritative filter through which the anti-Jewishness of the New Testament can be rendered null and void or, indeed, neutralized or even toned down. The New Testament antiJewish texts are very plain in what they say and, somehow, precisely because we do not live in the ancient historical context in which these texts were formulated -because these texts are uprooted from their first century context - these anti-Jewish sentiments have fermented over time so that today they may strike Christians listeners as far more compelling than they ever were even back in the first century.

The Church Fathers had the means for modifying the anti-Jewishness of the New Testament. Indeed, for reasons which are no longer operative today the Church Fathers intensified the damage to the point of possible irreparability, and the average Christian churchgoer is induced quite understandably to accept the New Testament's disparagement of the Jews at face value.

Accordingly, Jews distinguish between the Christian clergy and the Christian laity. While many Christian clergy have studied Scripture from the perspective of literary and source criticism, form and redaction criticism, and while many Christian clergy will declare without hesitation that not everything in the gospels is necessarily the "gospel truth", Jews believe that most of the Christian laity have absolutely no awareness that anti-Jewish animus in the New Testament should be understood in any way differently from what we read in the gospel texts themselves.

Jews are persuaded that most Christian churchgoers view Judaism through the anti-Jewish stereotypes that have often been implicit or implied in Christian theology: that Judaism is a religion of law in contrast to Christianity, a religion of love; that Judaism teaches "an eye for an eye and a tooth for a tooth" while Christianity teaches turning the other cheek; that the ancient Hebrew Patriarchs were forerunners of Christianity rather than of Judaism; that the God of Hebrew Scriptures is a God of justice, wrath, and vengeance rather than the New Testament God of love, grace, and forgiveness; that the trials which Jews have had to undergo throughout history are manifestations of their punishment at the hands of God for not accepting Jesus as divine. If there is any hope for future accomodation and understanding between Jews and Gentiles, we must together manage to put this stereotyping behind us at long last and involve the Christian churchgoer as well as the Christian clergy in this process.

I would like to see the learning process go two ways, with Jews learning more about Christianity and doing so sympathetically. Yet many Jews are impeded in this process by the associations which the name of Jesus calls to their attention. Many Jews involuntarily cringe when they hear the name of Jesus, since, over the centuries, Jews have been maimed and killed by those who have considered their actions to be in the name of Jesus. Tragically, because the name of Jesus has been enlisted in campaigns which have brought terror to Jewish history, Jews today may actually have lost the capacity to be responsive to the precious teachings imparted by the Jew Jesus.

What then has kept the door of dialogue ajar? One factor is the recognition that Jews and Christians are natural allies - that we need each other if we are to prevent a take-over by secularism, which has emerged as the powerful threat to all for which Judaism and Christianity stand. For many in our country, secularism has espoused self-gratification as a primary goal of existence, with fun and pleasure as indices of how alive one is. If allowed to build unchecked, the secular virtue of self-indulgence threatens our society with moral anarchy, a modern paganism potentially more corrosive of the values of Judaism and Christianity than many of the idolatries confronting our Prophets of old. Secularism is all the more sophisticated because it makes no demands and its idols are internalized.

For all the differences between those of us who are Christian and those of us who are Jewish, we both have so much more in common than either of us have with secularists-going-pagan. We both share an awareness that secularism can become a style of existence wherein people expose themselves as questing for a life of crude indulgence, of boastful achievement, of material accomplishment, a life based on transitory quests for transitory gains. Pleasure and property become our ultimate values, and people become slaves of anxiety, clinging to possessions because of the secret fear that they are slipping away.

Jews and Christians share the goal of remedying a society whose homes are deficient or devoid of religious values, a society whose young are often aimless and purposeless, fragile in their emotional health, unprepared for marriage and even for less serious types of relationship. Ours is the joint venture - that together we strive to bring new life to the myriads of persons in our own society who have never known the meaning of self-commitment, never achieved the capacity for faith or love, never understood or even glimpsed the nature of authentic life.

In essence, all of us, Christians and Jews alike, share in a theology of the "Kingdom of God," a Jewish concept whose basic message Jesus so poignantly captured, perpetuated, and embellished, a concept in the Jewish prayerbook to this day, where Jews pray in the following words:

> May the time not be distant, O God, when Thy name shall be worshipped in all the earth, when unbelief shall disappear and error be no more. Fervently we pray that the day may come when all men shall invoke Thy name, when corruption and evil shall give way to purity and goodness, when superstition shall no longer enslave the mind nor idolatry blind the eye, when all who dwell on earth shall know that to Thee alone every knee must bend and every tongue give homage.

> O may all, created in Thine image, recognize that they are brethren, so that, one in spirit and one in fellowship, they may be forever united before Thee. Then shall Thy kingdom be established on earth and the word of Thine ancient seer be fulfilled: The Lord will reign forever and ever. On that day the Lord shall be One and His name shall be One.[4]

NOTES

[1]Justin Martyr, Dialogue with Trypho, 16, 18.

[2]Ibid., Section 18.

[3]St. John Chrysostom, <u>Patrologia</u> <u>Graeca</u>, vol. 48, cols. 847-848 and 852.

[4]<u>The</u> <u>Union</u> <u>Prayer</u> <u>Book</u>, revised edition (New York: Central Conference of American Rabbis, 1961), p. 71.

CHAPTER TWO

THE JEWISH PEOPLE IN CHRISTIAN THEOLOGY: PRESENT AND FUTURE

Paul M. van Buren

Judaism in Christian Theology? In the past, Judaism has barely been in Christian theology at all, and insofar as it was, as Dr. Cook has described, it was present in strictly negative terms. That holds good from the earliest theological writing in the second century of the Common Era, up to the end of the first two thirds of the twentieth century. During this last third of the twentieth century, however, matters have begun to change, and as a result, a few Christian theologians are just beginning, here and there, to think about taking Judaism seriously and positively into Christian theology. This being the case, I shall only summarize briefly what has been said about Judaism in Christian theology, turn next to recent signs of change, and then spend most of my allotted time on the constructive task of outlining what it might be like if there were to be a genuine recognition and affirmation of Judaism within Christian theology, which, as I see it, is a moral prerequisite for any Christian theology after Auschwitz.

From its beginnings into the twentieth century, Christian theology, not bothering to distinguish between Judaism and the Jews, lumped both together in the category of things that ought not to exist. The Jews and their faithfulness to Torah represented a colossal failure on the part of God's former people to accept God's new revelation in Christ. They had therewith forfeited their inheritance (which has passed to the church) and they remained a negative witness to the consequences of human disobedience. For the sake of this negative and involuntary witness, the Jews were not to be killed, but neither were they to be allowed a normal place in Christian society. As soon as the church gained an effective upper hand over the empire, the Jews lost their citizenship and were increasingly denied civil rights. The only good Jew was the converted Jew, and even then he or she was to be watched with care. Only after the church lost its hold on the strings of political power did the Jews begin to regain normal political and human rights. But even an increasingly secularized, so-called Christian West still thought that an emancipated Jew should be baptized or at least stop practicing his Jewishness. As religious toleration spread, Christians relaxed their hostility to the Jews, but their theology did not change. The

Jews were still those who rejected Christ, were responsible for his death, and consequently carried a divine curse upon them in their wandering, homeless existence until the end of time, unless they gave up being Jews and became Christians. That is as mildly and charitably as it can be put, for no mention has been made of the murders and massacres of Jews by Christians, of which there were many. In the light of this history, it is easy enough to see how a contemporary Jewish thinker could say, "The only thing that we Jews want from Christians is that you keep your hands off of us and our children."

When one considers the longevity and stability of this teaching of contempt for Jews and Judaism, the signs of change over the past dozen years or so are astounding. Beginning with the Second Vatican Council, and especially since 1968, ecclesiastical bodies, councils of bishops and national church synods, both Catholic and Protestant, European and American, have begun speaking up on the subject with increasing penetration and clarity, and in such a way as to contradict this long teaching of anti-Judaism.

In 1970, to give one example, the Council of Bishops of the Dutch Catholic Church declared null and void a canon which they had passed as recently as 1924 urging Christians to have nothing to do with Jews. Now, they urged, in 1970, joint Bible study with them, and spoke of God's covenant with the Jews for all time. And in 1975 the National Council of Bishops in this country urged theologians begin to work on the task of exploring "the continuing relationship of the Jewish people with God." A collection of such statements, Protestant as well as Catholic, covering the post-World War II period up to 1975, runs to over one hundred and fifty pages of fairly small print.

It is not unusual to hear cries of "heresy" when groups of academics and intellectuals start to turn Christian teaching on its head. What is to be said when this is done by councils of Bishops and national church synods? I've never been much of a booster for ecclesiastical authority, but I must say that for once, at least, the leadership is well ahead of the rank and file, and I would recommend to any parish the study and discussion of what their leaders have been saying. These church leaders have reversed a tradition of over eighteen centuries for reasons which they name in some of these documents. The Holocaust and the emergence of the state of Israel, they say, are what have impelled them to speak in a new way about Jews and Judaism. It is my judgment that the emergence of the state of Israel was the more powerful of the two, for shameful as it is to confess it, more than one Christian leader was able to absorb the Holocaust into our traditional theology of the Jews as wandering, suffering, despised souls, paying forever for their stiff-necked rejection of Christ. What could not possibly fit into that mythical picture was the Israelis, holding out and winning their war of independence against the combined forces of five national armies. It is sobering to think that we have first begun to take the Jews seriously when they started acting like us--picking up a gun and shooting. Nevertheless, the Israeli Defense Force sweeping over the Sinai and retaking East Jerusalem was what could not possibly fit our traditional myth of the passive suffering Jew. The result is that events in modern Jewish history, perhaps as staggering as any in its whole history, have begun to reorient the minds of increasing numbers of responsible Christians.

Before turning to the constructive task of theological reflection on the reality of the Jewish people, let me pause to explore the first term of our subject--Judaism. Most Christians, if asked what they mean by Judaism probably would say; "the Jewish religion". Judaism would be to Jews, in this view, as Christianity is to Christians. But there is a real mistake here which is easy to uncover. Try this one: take away a Christian's Christianity, and what do you have? You have a pagan or a secularist. Take away a Jew's Judaism, and what do you have? A Jew. Jewishness is more than Judaism in a way that can't be understood on a Christian model. We can get at the heart of the matter by asking, what are Judaism's major concerns? The traditional answer is God, Torah, and Israel, the three great central affirmations of every type and branch of Judaism. The last of these terms warrants special attention by Christians. Judaism is concerned about the Jewish people - all the Jewish people, and all Jews as a people. They are not as concerned about the well-being of religious Jews or about the support of the synagogue as much as they are about the well-being of the Jewish people. So, if we Christians want to take Judaism seriously in its own terms, we shall learn to talk about the Jewish people, not Judaism. Judaism is an aspect of the whole and exists for the sake of the whole reality of the Jewish people. The issue before us, therefore, is not Christianity and Judaism; the issue is the Church and the Jewish people. Our topic, then, to rephrase it so as to meet the self-definition of both sides and the actual task before us, is the Jewish people in the church's theology.

If there is to be a positive place for the Jewish people within the church's theology, what will be the consequences? I should like to develop the essentials of such a theology around four topics or doctrines: ecclesiology that is, our understanding of the church, of ourselves; the doctrine of the Trinity or our understanding of God; the doctrine of Christology--or our understanding of Jesus Christ; and finally the doctrine of revelation--or our understanding of how we come to understand all this.

I

If Christians come to a new understanding of Blacks, of women, of native Americans (and there has been considerable development in each of these in recent years) these insights call for subtle and important shifts in other areas of their understanding. If they come to a new understanding of the Jewish people, however, the whole picture will come to look different. I want to assure the nervous among my fellow Christians, that it will be recognizably the same picture, but a shift at this particular point touches every other point and forces shifts in each.

Why is this so? Why are the Jews such a special case for the church and its theology? If one will recall how the church began, the answer is not hard to come by. It just happens to be a formative fact for the church, that Jesus of Nazareth was a Jew. Mary, his mother was a Jew. Peter, Andrew, James, John, all of his disciples without exception were Jews, as was that somewhat special apostle, Paul. The Gospel of John, for reasons that perhaps tell us much more about the situation of its author than about the time of Jesus, said of Jesus in the prologue, that "he came unto his own, and his own received him not." Happily, that is not true. Were not Mary and Joseph his own? And Peter and Andrew and James and John and all the rest of his followers? Had none of them received him, the Gospel of John would never have been written. Since I am happy to be a Christian, and therefore happy that there is the Gospel of John, I am all the more happy that on this crucial point that Gospel is wrong.

Because Jesus was a Jew and his environment was the Jewish people, the movement which came to be the Christian church began as a Jewish sect. It saw itself as a renewal of Israel, and it worked out its self-understanding as an interpretation of Israel's Scripture. Like many another sect, its members were convinced that they had the true interpretation of their own Jewish tradition in contrast to their neighbors, that is, the other Jews. In short, what we call the first Christians saw themselves as the truest of true Jews. The Jesus-movement grew first entirely among Jews. Very shortly, however, and as a most startling and unsettling development, they found proselytes, then Gentiles, flocking to join them. Within several generations, this little Jewish sect was on its way to becoming a largely Gentile enterprise, and by the end of the second century, it had become almost exclusively that. As it became less Jewish, it developed its self-understanding as a community which had displaced the Jews as God's elect. It claimed Israel's tradition as its own, Israel's Scriptures as its own Holy Writ, Israel's God as its God. As a consequence, the church's selfunderstanding has, from its very beginning and ever since, involved also an understanding of the Jews. It follows, therefore, that if the church is changing its views of the Jewish people as radically as its leaders are now demanding, then its own self-understanding will inevitably be changed.

Historians of Christian origins are coming to the new conclusion that Catholic Christianity and Rabbinic Judaism are twins-exact contemporaries. Both were born in the first century, one following the Rabbi of Nazareth, and the other following Rabbi Johanan Ben Zakkai (who had also worked for a while in another Galilean town some twenty miles to the south of Nazareth and at about the same time as Jesus, but who had out-lived the siege and destruction of Jerusalem forty years later, and as an old man began the Academy in the town of Javneh, from which developed Rabbinic Judaism). Both movements claim the same Father, and both were the children of one mother. That one mother was the post-exilic implimentation of Ezra's reform by the Pharisees. All those nasty things said about Pharisees in our Gospels reflect the later split between the young church and the young Rabbinic Judaism. They mask the evidence in their own sources that the Jesus-movement was,in its origins, an offshoot of Pharisaic Judaism.

Not only were those two siblings born together of the same mother, they grew, expanded, and reached maturity at almost exactly the same time. By the end of the fifth century C.E., Catholic Christianity had given definitive shape to its doctrine, form and life, and Rabbinic Judaism had completed the compilation of the Talmud, refining the form of life which has kept the Jewish people going unto our own day. The two siblings developed in almost total disregard of each other, but the parallel is remarkable. In psychological terms, then, the Jewish people is for the church its most special and significant other. No other people, no other group, no other religion bears even a faint reflection of this relationship for the church. If the church stops thinking of the Jews as the rejected remnant of the people Israel, if it starts speaking of the continuing covenantal relationship between this people and God, then it will have to rethink its own identity.

So who are we Christians? If, as we are now beginning to say, the Jewish people are the people of God, then who are we? Well, as I look around at my fellow Christians, one thing is evident. Whatever we are, we aren't Jews. Here and there you may come across a Christian of Jewish background, but the exception proves the rule. We Christians are, in overwhelming preponderance, Gentiles. Now a Gentile is, by definition, a non-Jew. Given the difficulty of defining just who or what a Jew is, that means we define ourselves in terms of that which is indefinable, which hardly makes for conceptual neatness. Nevertheless, the fact is obvious once we get the Jewish people in focus, we can see that we Christians are not Jews, not God's Israel, not the people of God. What are we then? We are just what we have always said; we are God's church. Only now we may and must add, that we are God's Gentile church. The church may have begun as a purely Jewish movement, but within not many generations, it had become what it has remained ever since - a predominantly Gentile enterprise.

We can be more specific: We are Gentiles, but we are not all the Gentiles. Most of the Gentiles - that is, most people of this world who are not Jews - are not Christians either. We are only some of the Gentiles, a church called out from all the nations. And we are distinguished from all the other Gentiles by one fact and by one fact only: We are Gentiles who worship the God of the Jews, the Holy One of Israel, blessed be He.

The Jews, it should be added, have always known and praised their God as theirs but also as the King of the Universe. God and Lord of all. Just this God is the one they also know intimately as the Father, as the giver of Torah, as One who has entered into a special relationship of love with the chosen people. And just this same One is the God whom we Christians worship, the God of Abraham, Isaac, and Jacob, the giver of the commandments on Sinai, the God of the Hebrew Scriptures, whom Jesus and every faithful Jew knew and know as Father. So when I say that we worship the God of the Jews, I am only sharpening what has always been acknowledged in general terms in our theology; I am not saying anything all that new.

Not only are we Gentiles who worship the God of the Jews, but we do so with a vocabulary and with concepts which are predominantly Jewish. Listen to yourselves, my fellow Gentile Christians, and be amazed! We speak of creation and covenant, of sin and forgiveness, of righteousness and loving kindness, or revelation and redemption, of resurrection and the world to come. Those are all Jewish terms and concepts, used by Jews before ever there was a church, and used by Jews to this day. Without our use of this translated Jewish vocabulary, we would have almost nothing to say as Christians. Remove that vocabulary, and we destroy our prayers, our worship, and our Eucharist. Think only of the Psalter, the primary prayer book of the church. The reason for our use of this language is obvious. We carry with us and hold sacred the holy Scriptures of the Jewish people. We have often differed with them as to its meaning, but then we have often differed among ourselves as to its meaning, but by accepting this book as our sacred Scripture, we acknowledge the right and power of this book to interpret us. In the midst of all of our differences in trying to interpret it, it addresses us in all our differences, including our differences with Jews, and it challenges us to come to a better understanding and especially a better form of life in obedience to the God of whom it speaks.

If the Hebrew Scriptures have one central and enduring subject, it is Israel, the people of God. The Jewish people and their ancestors are not only those who wrote and preserved the Scriptures; they are also its protagonists. One who reads the Scriptures reads of Abraham, Isaac, and Jacob – yes, and of Sarah, Rebecca, and Rachel – of Moses and David, of the kings and prophets, and this is the book we hold as sacred. We have, of course, added other books. The Apostolic Writings, usually called the New Testament, presents itself as an interpretation of the Hebrew Scriptures. Much of its story of Jesus is told by piecing together quotations from Scriptures, and all of it is presented as being "according to the Scriptures," as its authors often put it. So with the Jewish book as our first holy Scriptures, and so with Jewish vocabulary and concepts, we are Gentiles who worship the God of the Jews as also our God.

We do so as Gentiles. We are not Jews. We do so as God's beloved and elect church, not as God's beloved and elect people. So we do this in our own Gentile way. We have developed our own forms of worship and prayer. We have added our Apostolic Writings and bound them together with the Scriptures as our sacred book. We have our own form of life and our own church structure. They have their Sabbath, and we have our Sunday, which is not the Sabbath, but the weekly celebration of Easter. We do not imitate the Jews, nor should we. It is one thing to be invited as a guest of the Jewish family to celebrate their Passover Seder. That is fine. It would be quite another matter for a Christian congregation to celebrate the Passover Seder as its own. That would be to break the eighth commandment – Thou shalt not steal. Moreover, it would be to question the wisdom and purpose of God, who has called into being not only his beloved people the Jews, but also his beloved Gentile church, both for the sake of the completion of creation.

This raises an issue of the greatest importance: what are we to make of this strange development out of the reform of Ezra and the work of the Pharisees? What are we to say to this development of the Gentile church out of a Jewish sect, accompanied as it was by a flowering of Judaism that matches any from its long history? Because we have been schooled in Israel's Scripture, we know what we shall say: Surely the hand of the Lord was in these developments, often in ways which we knew not. It is, we shall say, evidently the will of the holy One of Israel, that that greatest of all love affairs of history between God and God's people continue, but that God provides also a way for Gentiles, as Gentiles, to enter along with the chosen people into the task of taking responsibility for moving this unfinished creation nearer to its completion.

The alternative is to call it all a great mistake – not a development according to the will of God. In effect, that is

what both sides have done from the latter part of the first
century up until well into the twentieth.   But if we take
Judaism into Christian theology - really into it - we cannot
repeat the old answer that Judaism should have faded away.
And if we maintain a different answer for a few hundred years,
maybe the Jews will have grounds someday, for the first time
in their history, to bless the God of Israel who has also
called the Gentile church to work alongside of them in the
awesome task of hastening the completion of this threatened
creation.   That is, after all, what is at stake.   Creation is
in great danger.   What God began in the beginning was good,
very good, but it was only a good beginning.   Creation is
still incomplete, and so in danger of not making it.   That is
why it is so important that Jews engage in Torah and
Christians follow Christ.   When Jews engage in Torah and when
Christians follow Christ, they are practicing, here in this
incomplete creation, their baby steps for walking in the age
of creation's completion, in the age of Messiah.   In doing so
they hope to hasten the coming of that age.   That is a great
responsibility.   We Christians and Jews really do exist for
the sake of the world, and that means also for the sake of the
world that is coming.

                                II

        I should like to turn now to that most distinctively
Christian doctrine, the doctrine of the Trinity.   With our
eyes on the reality of the Jewish people, and so with a
realistic sense of our own Gentile identity, it becomes immediately evident that this doctrine is absolutely essential and
central to the church, because it expresses so clearly the
peculiarly Gentile apprehension of the God of Israel.   Jews
are often upset by this doctrine because they think it
threatens the unity of God, but they are forgetting that this
is our Gentile confession.   The Jews can and do confess God in
the words of the Shema, "Hear, oh Israel, the Lord our God,
the Lord is one," or unique.   But the doctrine of the triune
God does not seek to say anything other than this - it only
says it in a Gentile way.

        In order to make this clear, we need to begin with the
aspect of this teaching about God that touches our Gentile
apprehension of Him most directly —God as Spirit.   When we say
that God is Spirit, we are confessing the miracle of the God
of Israel having reached out and gathered in a Gentile church.
And we must start here because apart from this miracle, we
Gentiles would not be talking about the God of Israel at all.
And when we say not just the Spirit that comes from God, or
the Spirit as an agency of God, but that the Holy Spirit just
is the God of Israel, we confess that God has done this thing,
the God of Abraham, Isaac and Jacob, the God of the Jews.   God

has willed and effected, that along with His beloved people, there should also be His beloved Gentile church, serving God and the plan for the completion and sanctification of creation. That is what we are claiming when we confess God to be also Holy Spirit. God hovered over His new creation, called Abraham, gave Torah to the chosen people, and spoke by the prophets. Now God has done this new thing of calling together the Gentile church. We believe, we must believe - in God the Holy Spirit.

That hardly makes two Gods. What is misleading here is that the words in Greek and Latin with which this teaching was worked out were translated into an early form of English that turns into a total mistranslation in modern English. To speak of God in three persons in modern English can only mean three Gods, for persons are individuals. But that is certainly not what the Latin "persona" meant, nor the original Greek word. The term the Greek Fathers used meant "a way of being (God)". God, they were saying, was completely and fully God in doing this new thing of reaching out and gathering His church to service. So we would do well to drop the word 'person' from the doctrine of the Trinity if we want to be loyal to the Church Fathers and especially if we want to be faithful to God. The God whom we confess as Holy Spirit is the Ruler, the one God of Israel, beside whom there is no other.

By the Spirit, then, we Gentiles confess the one God of Israel, but we do so through Jesus Christ. It has been given to the Jewish people by the covenant of Sinai to stand, if they so choose, in an immediate relationship to God, who for this reason allows Himself to be designated "God of Israel". Every Jew is authorized to call upon God as Father, for Israel has been designated God's child by God. Not so the other nations. The prophet Zechariah had a glimpse of how the Gentiles would come to know God when he wrote, "In those days ten men from the nations of every tongue will take hold of the robe of a Jew saying let us go with you, for we have heard that God is with you." (Zechariah 8:23) As a matter of fact, there was one Jew, one of God's many childlren in Israel, who so lived the intimacy of his people with God that many sensed that in him some new step was to be taken in God's plan to bring His creation nearer to its completion.

I shall have more to say shortly about what happened to this Jew and what his followers came to say about him. For the moment, suffice it to say that this one man became the Jew to whose robe hundreds and thousands and millions of Gentiles have been able to take hold and go with him to his Father. Of all God's Jewish sons, no wonder the Gentiles call this one God's Son with a capital "S". And that is why we pray all our prayers to God through Jesus Christ our Lord, for, we believe, God has given us Gentiles this Jew to be our ruler and master as our way to Him.

For the Jewish people, Moses is and remains first among them, for by his hands God gave them Torah, instruction to be received with joy in how to begin already now to practice walking in the coming days of Messiah. For Christians, however, Jesus stands alone, for he is the one Jew whom we believe God has used as our mediator, so that Gentiles though we may be, we may yet hear through this Jew God's word of love for us Gentiles.

You may have heard it said that Jesus is God. That hardly does justice to Orthodox Christian teaching. Jesus was a Jew, a human being, a first century Palestinian preacher and healer. Christian teaching, is that God's word for us Gentiles is heard by us in this man, that the God of Israel confronts us Gentiles in this Jew, that this Jew and Israel's God are so united in this work of bringing Gentiles to God's service, that when we Gentiles look at this Jew, we see all we can and all we need to see of the God of Abraham, Isaac and Jacob. That is why we say that God's word spoken to us in this man is no other than the very word of God the God whose word is good, the holy One of Israel.

So it is that our doctrine of the Trinity really does express our peculiarly Gentile apprehension of the God of the Jews. It may seem a bit complicated but, after all, the fact of Gentiles worshipping the God of the Jews is not all that simple or obvious a matter. All I have done in these remarks on the doctrine of the Trinity is to lay out the classical Christian doctrine with only shifts of emphasis and expression which follow from taking Judaism seriously and positively into Christian theology. Such shifts are necessary, but they take away nothing that has been traditionally at the heart of Christian faith.

III

This brings us to the very heart of that faith, namely, that which took place in the life, death and resurrection of Jesus of Nazareth. If we Christians are going to take Judaism seriously and positively into Christian theology, then perhaps the best way to begin here is to point out the obvious historical fact that already in the Apostolic Writings, and certainly down through the history of Christian theology, the word "Christ" has been used as a proper name. We have called the man from Nazareth "Jesus Christ", and we, his followers, have been called and call ourselves "Christians". The word "Christ" was, at first, the Greek translation of the Hebrew <u>mashiah</u>—Messiah, but it had that meaning only as long as the Jesus-movement remained a Jewish sect, which was not for long. If you want to ask the Jewish question about Messiah, then stick with the Jewish term and its proper Jewish meaning. The concept of mashiah was not well-fixed in the first century, but roughly speaking, he was the figure who either inaugurated or was closely associated with the beginning of the Messianic age. Quite a number of people down through history have been thought by some Jews to have been the Messiah. But there is a simple way to find out if they were right about this. The Jewish rule is: no Messianic age, no Messiah. Since I don't recall in the past nor see in the present that the nations are exactly lining up to beat their swords into plowshares or their spears into pruning hooks, I think I can safely and honestly conclude that the Messianic age has not arrived and so that the Messiah is yet to appear. So my subject is Christology, not Messiology, a topic in Christian theology, not Jewish theology.

This is not to deny that some of Jesus' first followers, perhaps before but certainly after Easter, thought and claimed that he was the Messiah. They were first century Jews living under Roman oppression and the Jewish hope for a liberating Messiah was the greatest hope they had. So they tied their greatest hope to the greatest person they knew in the only terms they had. That is quite understandable but it is clearly a matter calling for further interpretation in the light of further history. The Messianic Age did not arrive, and other events occurred of which those first disciples never dreamed in those early days of the Movement. What is not at all clear is whether Jesus himself ever thought of himself as the Messiah. The scholars of the problem whose arguments I find most convincing conclude that probably he did not - that at most he did not deny the charge at his inquisition before Pilate - but we shall never know for sure. What seems reasonably certain is that Pilate thought that Jesus was a messianic pretender, for he had him executed under the title "King of the Jews," which is probably as close as that Roman tyrant could have come to understanding a Jewish concept. And then a strange thing happened. A crucified Messiah must have seemed the ultimate contradiction in terms for those Jews who had followed Jesus and surely the distressing end of the story. But within a few days those same disciples were proclaiming in public that God had exalted ·Jesus, that he was alive and blessed by God. As historians we shall never uncover what happened, for what happened, it was claimed, was God's act, and that is not a category with which historians can deal without wrecking their discipline. The judgement we make about Easter is a judgement of faith and, therefore, one having consequences for our existence. It is one which a Jew need not make. It is one which the Christian makes necessarily upon becoming a Christian.

The Christian judgement is that he who was crucified as King of the Jews has become the royal Jew for us Gentiles. God's plan to bring creation nearer to its completion with this man was cut short by the intervention of a Gentile,

Pontius Pilate. But Easter, so we Christians have discovered, was God's act to turn that cruel Gentile act into a blessing for countless Gentiles, so that by the murder of this one Jew, we who were "alienated" from the commonwealth of Israel and strangers to the covenants of promise, having no hope and without God in the world," (to quote the so-called Letter to the Ephesians), "now in Christ Jesus," we "who were once far off have been brought near in the blood of Christ." Near to what? Near to the God who is bound forever to the people Israel, therefore, near to the Jewish people. He or she who is not near to the Jewish people cannot be near to the God and Father of Jesus of Nazareth. That is the logic of the cross to which we have for so long been blind.

Christians have developed as many interpretations of the cross as Jews have of the Messiah. A first and obvious view- obvious in the light of the fact that the first interpreters were all Temple-going Jews - was to think of it as a Temple- like sacrifice for sin. If the Temple cult really speaks to you, that is one possibility. Personally and as a Gentile, I find more sustenance in seeing it as an act of political oppression that can invite us Gentiles into the service of the God of justice, and to learn from the Scriptures what real justice is all about, and how it has to be combined with mercy. However interpreted, the cross has been our central Christian symbol for the evident reason that this man's death, affirmed as precious to God by what happened on Easter, is the reason why Christians have dared to believe they have the right to call upon and serve the God of Israel as truly their God, through Jesus Christ their Lord.

And in the end? Can we picture the end, the completion of creation, when He who became the Creator will have also become the Redeemer? The apostle Paul made two attempts to do so, and in each God stands alone as Redeemer without any reference to Christ. One of these is in Romans 11, and the other and more explicit is in 1 Corinthians 15. In the Corinthian letter, Paul's vision of the end is preceded by Christ stepping out of the picture, so that God can be "all in all", whatever that may mean. Neither here nor in Romans 11, where Paul dealt explicitly with the relationship between the church and the Jewish people, did he say everyone would become a Christian in the end. What he did see instead was all creation adoring its Creator, and that's not a false picture in Jewish eschatology either.

As for our Christology, we have always said in our theology that Jesus was the embodiment of the word of his Father, not an independent word on his own. What could be more like him as he is presented by the apostolic authors than that he step aside, once he has brought us Gentiles to our knees before his God, the God of Israel? I think Paul had it about right.

IV

Finally, we are going to be led into some fresh thinking about revelation and the Bible, if we are to take Judaism seriously into Christian theology. Let me begin with the Bible. As you may have noticed, I have been calling the two parts of the book which we carry through history "the Scriptures" and "the Apostolic Writings", rather than the Old Testament and the New Testament. I do so because I want to avoid implying the insidious comparison of the Old/New distinction, and because for Jesus and the apostles, the sacred writings of Israel were called simply "the Scriptures". This was the church's first Bible, and the writings coming out of the apostolic communities were largely midrashim, imaginative interpretations of those Scriptures. Those interpretations of the sacred tradition were made in the light of the events of the time. They reflect on every page the situation of the authors and the communities that produced them. They do so because the authors thought that since history matters to God, it should matter to them. They believed that they were living in a world which belonged to God and that the course of the events of their time were in some way part of God's developing history with creation. So the tremendous influx of Gentiles into the young Jesus-movement, the war with Rome and its terrible conclusion in the sack of Jerusalem and the destruction of the Temple in the year 70 C.E., then somewhere about 85 C.E., the exclusion of members of the Jesus movement from the synagogue and the accompanying growing hostility between the church and the synagogue - all this was taken to be part of God's history with creation as it moved it towards its completion.

Now the question that is before us today is what are we to make of this element of hostility in the Apostolic Writings, reflecting the situation at the time of their composition. It is undeniably there, but then, so is the long history of the past nineteen centuries undeniably there. If we share with the authors of our Apostolic Writings the conviction that God's history with His creation is still taking place, that this world still matters to God, then should we not put that hostility in its historical context and make up our minds before God and develop our own midrash, as did the apostles, in the light of what has happened? I suggest that just exactly this is what has been going on to lead to the new interpretation of our tradition by church leaders to which I referred at the beginning of this lecture.

Let us look at this matter from another angle. Recent events in the history of the Jewish people have impelled church leaders to reinterpret our tradition, and that involves, not least, reading the Apostolic Writings with new eyes. Note what is happening to us here. Those Apostolic

Writings were themselves reinterpretations of Israel's tradition in response to what were, for their authors, recent events in Jewish history. Not only that, but the Scriptures in turn which the apostolic authors reinterpreted were themselves the product of a long history of reinterpretation upon reinterpretation of Israel's own tradition, always in the light of ever new events in Israel's history. At this point we had better move with the greatest care, for we are approaching the human side -and there has always been this human side - of the foundation of both Judaism and Christianity. The tradition has a name for it: revelation. We are standing before the human side - and there has been a human side - of God's Let us therefore remove our sandals and proceed slowly, step by step, for this is holy ground.

On the human side of this holy ground, at least since Abraham, there has always been tradition. For Moses before the burning bush and again at Sinai, the One revealed was already the God of the Patriarchs. For the prophets this was the God of the Exodus and Sinai, of David and Mt. Zion. For the apostles this was always the God of Israel. Behind them and behind us, by way of the apostles and Church Fathers for the church, and by way of the men of Great Assembly and the Rabbis for the Jewish history. There has always been tradition. But then, over against or in the context of this tradition, there have occurred new and unexpected events in Jewish history. Note well that these were events specifically in _Jewish_ history. How Pharoah treated his other slaves, we do not know. What matters for revelation is how he treated his Jewish slaves. Historians may know something of how Cyrus treated his other captives, but for revelation, only his decree about the Jews counts. Roman governors and procuratous crucified any number of suspected insurrectionists in the first century; for the story of revelation, only his crucifixion of the Galilean Jew in Jerusalem made the difference. Not every event in Jewish history has had this effect, but only those events which were part of Jewish history have had the reorienting effect of producing reinterpretations of Israel's tradition which are the human face of revelation.

That brings us to the decisive moment. Given the tradition and in response to new events in Jewish history, one or more persons have been lead to reinterpret the tradition so as to lead up to and include the latest events of God's dealing with His creation, thereby coming to a new apprehension of God and His will for us. So it was with Moses, with Amos, with Second Isaiah, and with the apostles, and so it would appear to be happening to our church leaders over those past dozen years, nor is it happening only to us Christians. Emil Fackenheim, no minor figure on the Jewish side, has spoken of what he calls "a commanding voice from Auschwitz," and that is unmistakably the language of revelation.

If this is indeed what is happening, it means that the history of revelation is still going on. It means that God is by no means finished with either the chosen people or the church. It means that the story is not over, not all in the past. It means, all other evidence to the contrary, Emmanuel - "God with us". God with us, right in the events of the most recent history of God's holy people. Can we really say that? Can we, who first learned to see this in a Jew dying in agony on a Gentile cross, see this in the brothers and sisters of that Jew who were gassed and burned in Auschwitz? For if today we cannot see God suffering there with the chosen people, what possible right have we Christians to go on saying that God suffered there with one whose dying word was "forsaken"? And yet if we can see this, we are looking at the bitter fact of the failure of Christians - yes, of the judgement of God upon the church. For we were there when they crucified the brothers and sisters of our Lord, the least of his brothers and sisters, and we did next to nothing to help. "In as much as you did it not to one of the least of these my brothers you did it not to me." If Emmanuel, God with us, then God help us!

One thing is certain: After Auschwitz, nothing in our hearts or our theology, if we would be disciples of our Lord Jesus, the Jew from Nazareth, can be as it was before, and any word or act that we Gentiles do that separates us from the least of his Jewish brothers and sisters, stands under the judgement of Auschwitz, and therefore under the judgement of the cross. "As you do it to the least of these my brothers" -and please no spiritualizing, no mystifying typology, his real flesh and blood Jewish brothers - "you do it to me." My fellow Gentiles, how strange it is that you and I dare to pray to the God of the Jews, to the one who willed to be known as the holy One of Israel. So when you pray, remember that the Jewish people prayed in Auschwitz as they went to the gas chambers, for had they not, what possibility of prayer would remain? The possibility, however, is there, and therefore we Gentiles can and may pray to the God of Israel. This means, moreover, that God's history with the beloved people, the beloved church, and the beloved world has not stopped, and that we are living at a turning point in God's history with us, which is also our history with God. That too is part of what we shall see when we finally find the proper place for Judaism and the Jewish people within Christian theology.

PART TWO:

THE JEWISH PEOPLE IN CHRISTIAN PREACHING

CHAPTER THREE

THE JEWISH PEOPLE IN CHRISTIAN PREACHING: A CATHOLIC
PERSPECTIVE

Eugene Fisher

This paper is presented, centrally but not exclusively, from the point of view of one who is a Roman Catholic Christian: "centrally" because that is what I am (not just "happen to be") and Catholicism is the tradition which has shaped my experience and thought patterns;[1] "not exclusively" because the problems we Christians face in cleaning up the shameful "teaching of contempt"[2] we have projected on the Jews for the past two millenia cuts across, and beneath, all denominational barriers. As A. Roy Eckardt succinctly puts it: "Opposition to Jews is the one constant of Christian history."[3] The 1974 Vatican Guidelines state it in a more positive way: "The problem of Jewish-Christian relations concerns the Church as such, since it is when 'pondering her own mystery' that she encounters the mystery of Israel."[4]

The issues we must grapple with today are thus not simply questions of neighborliness or "being nice" to each other. For the Christian, they involve radical faith-issues as well. In the process of dialogue, we encounter ourselves on the deepest spiritual level and ask: "Who am I, as a Christian, and why?"

Such questions, of course, lie at the core of what it means to preach the gospel. To the extent that our proclamation of the kerygma is influenced by the false polemics of the past, to that extent are we missing or perverting our essential mission as preachers of God's Word.

Negative Successes

The problem faced by the preacher in striving for a prejudice-free proclamation of the Good News are quite obviously related to (indeed flow from) those faced by the theologian and the exegete. Perhaps our present situation can be clarified if we view what is needed as a two-pronged

effort, with both prongs equally critical for over-all success.

One pole, the negative, aims at the past, at clarifying
and eradicating the hydra-headed monster of antisemitism which
has enwrapped itself around Christian preaching almost from
the beginning and most certainly from the time of the Fathers
of the Church.[5]

Thus far we Christians have had reasonable success in
achieving this negative, corrective goal. My own study of
current Roman Catholic teaching materials,[6] for example,
measured signigicant improvement in the treatment of Jews and
Judaism compared with the results of studies of Catholic texts
done in the early 1960's.[7] Whole chunks of the traditional
polemic, such as the "divine retribution" theory (i.e. that
Jewish suffering is willed by God in punishment for an alleged
"rejection" of Jesus), have virtually disappeared from our
religious vocabulary. And, with the exception of passages
dealing with the Pharisees and the Crucifixion, blatant
stereotyping of Jews can also be said to be a thing of the
past. The Crusades and the Inquisition, when mentioned, are
clearly condemned. The Jewishness of Jesus and the Jewish
heritage of Christian liturgical practices are highlighted
with increasing frequency.

What is remarkable about this achievement, of course, is
the brevity of time in which it occurred. When placed in
relief against almost two millenia of vituperation, the change
wrought in Catholic teaching by the Second Vatican Council in
the past decade and a half has been little short of the mira-
culous.

In negative terms, then, Christian reaction to the implications of the Holocaust can be viewed as acceptable, if
incomplete. We have analyzed and excised many of the major
elements of the old polemic and begun well the task of
dismantling the teaching of contempt. We know where we are,
and to a real extent what we still need to do to get where we
want to go.

For the liturgist and the preacher, the task on this
score is at least beginning to be clear. Official statements
from a wide variety of churches[8] have already pinpointed the
major issues and the direction that needs to be taken. The
following excerpts from the 1974 Vatican Guidelines give some
specifics:

> With respect to liturgical readings, care will be
> taken to see that homilies based on them will not
> distort their meaning, especially when it is a
> question of passages which seem to show the Jewish
> people as such in an unfavorable light. Efforts will

be made so to instruct the Christian people that they will understand the true interpretation of all the texts and their meaning for the contemporary believer.

---Judaism in the time of Christ and the Apostles was a complex reality, embracing many different trends, many spiritual, religious, social, and cultural values; ---The Old Testament and the Jewish tradition founded upon it must not be set against the New Testament in such a way that the former seems to constitute a religion of only justice, fear and legalism, with no appeal to the love of God and neighbor (cf. Deut. 6:5, Lev. 19:18, Matt. 22:34-40).

---With regard to the trial and death of Jesus, the Council recalled that "what happened in his passion cannot be blamed upon all the Jews then living, without distinction, nor upon the Jews of today" (Nostra Aetate, 4).

---The history of Judaism did not end with the destruction of Jerusalem, but rather went on to develop a religious tradition. And, although we believe that the importance and meaning of that tradition were deeply affected by the coming of Christ, it is still nonetheless rich in religious values.[9]

The difficulties of achieving such ends from the pulpit should not be underestimated. Holy Week, for example, offers a major challenge to the ingenuity of the most skillful homilist. The misunderstandings surrounding the actual events of Jesus' passion and death are so deeply ingrained in our hearers (and often enough in ourselves) that only a major effort combining all of the Church's educational resources (the classroom, the pulpit, and even the Sunday bulletin) will turn the tide.[10]

Yet, given our knowledge of the history of Christian antisemitism, we dare not presume that the Christian will leave our present Holy Week liturgies with anything other than a distorted, negative attitude toward Jews and Judaism. It is the preacher who most make the conscious effort to combat the negative stereotypes that can arise today unless the Scriptual texts of this period are carefully explained in the light of the best current scholarship.[11]

Examples of New Testament passages that can give rise to misunderstandings about Jews and Judaism range from the obvious to the subtle. In the former category are to be found, among others, those texts depicting the Pharisees as religious hypocrites. Here, the danger lies not simply in a distorted view of Phariasaism alone. There is a dynamic embedded in the Christian consciousness, which tends to transfer negatives from individual Pharisees to the Pharisees as a whole, from the Pharisees to all the Jews of Jesus' time, and finally to all Jews of all times. One winds up, often without conscious reflection, ascribing to Judaism as such, and to all Jews, specific characteristics (such as materialism and legalism) not applicable even to the Pharisees as a group.

Jesus, as we know today, was highly Pharisaical in his teachings. The Sermon on the Mount, for example, conforms both in its general tone and in its particulars to the teachings of the Pharisees as reflected in rabbinic literature.[11] And quite often passages which seem to portray Jesus in opposition to the Pharisees as a whole turn out, on closer examination, to be cases in which Jesus, as a pious Jew active in the life of his community, is participating in an internal debate then going on within the richly multifaceted Pharisaic movement of his time. Jesus' dictum on the Sabbath preserved in Mark 2:27, for example, is quite similar to that ascribed to Hillel, who lived in the century before Jesus: "The Sabbath is committed to you, you are not committed to the Sabbath" (Mekilta 31:13). The Mishnah (Shabbath 128a)reveals a controversy between the school of Hillel and that of Shamai on whether plucking "corn" by hand violates the Sabbath. Jesus appears to side with the ruling of Hillel that only "winnowing" and "grinding" with tools constitutes a form of labor that would break the Sabbath rest.

Much of the bitterness toward the Pharisees to be found in Matthew's gospel, preachers should point out, actually reflects the controversies of Matthew's (much later) times rather than the situation that existed between Jesus and his people in his own lifetime. This bitterness need not be hidden. It exists in the text. But it does need to be understood for what it is, lest serious misunderstandings of the essential gospel message result.

Christians need to know the history of the writing of the sacred texts which are proclaimed in the liturgy. By the time Matthew and John came to write their versions in the last decades of the first century, for example, the Temple had already been destroyed, and the close relations that had earlier prevailed between Christians and their fellow Jews had been strained to the breaking point. Matthew and John both reflect the feelings of their communities on what they viewed as a virtual expulsion from the synagogue (Mt. 5:10-12; 20:16-33; 22:6; 23:29-99; John 9:22; 12:42; 16:2).

Any comparison between parallel passages from the earlier (Mark & Luke) to the later (Matthew & John) gospels shows how the rhetoric concerning the Jews escalated in response to the historic events surrounding the split between Christianity and its parent religious community. Matthew's version of the parables of the Tenants (Mt. 21; compare Mk. 12; Lk. 20) and the Wedding Feast (Mt. 22, compare Lk. 14) have Jews being punished and even killed by God, seemingly to be replaced by Gentile Christians. These are images of violence not found in the earlier sources. Matthew's passion likewise escalates the defense of Pilate, who is known from history as a blood tyrant. Matthew's inventive insertions into the text, such as the famous line: "And all the people answered: his blood be upon us and upon our children" (Mt. 27:25) functioned polemically against the Jews encountered by the Matthean community at the end of the 1st Century.

Such passages have caused untold generations of Christians to emerge from our Churches during Holy Week with hatred toward Jews in their hearts, a hatred that all too often has manifested itself in vicious programs and other persecutions. Such, surely, was not the intent of the Biblical author. High rhetoric was the order of the day, especially for writers who, like the New Testament authors, were deeply immersed in the high level of rhetoric of the Hebrew Scriptures, especially the prophets on whom they so often drew. The gospels preach love, not hate. It was later Christian generations that, become increasingly "Gentilized", forgot the original historical context of the New Testament and lost the intimate awareness of Judaism that its authors presumed in their hearers. Without a deep awareness of the authenic Jewish context, and a respect for Judaism such as Jews and the Apostles themselves held, the gospel message can be turned upside down (literally perverted) - from love to hate. It is, I would argue, an essential role of the homilist to set the gospels back into their historical context today by the full use of the insights of modern biblical scholarship.

A closely related issue which deserves the urgent attention of liturgists is suggested by the Vatican Guidelines. It deserves mention here, if only for the sake of completeness in this brief survey of needed liturgical correctives.

As is becoming increasingly accepted among biblical scholars, the anti-Jewish polemic, occasioned by the bitterness of the split between Christianity and Judaism in the first century, extends far beyond the Passion Narratives and the more obviously hostile passages such as Matthew 23. Throughout his gospel, for example, Matthew alters or makes additions to his sources to further his polemic against the Pharisees of his own time.[12] The speeches in the Acts of the Apostles, (such as Stephen's in Acts 7 and Paul's in Acts 13) even where they once seemed to be nothing more than a neutral history of Israel" (Dibelius), are being revealed by modern scholarship to be essentially polemical.[13] And the majority of uses of the term 'Ioudaios' in John's gospel reflect hostilities current within the Johannine community at the time of the gospel's being written down rather than any actual historical reference to the Jewish community of Jesus' time. While the term 'Ioudaios'appears some 71 times in the Fourth gospel, in only 23 cases does it have a neutral, historical sense.[14] In the remainder of the passages, it has one or another of a range of hostile, polemic connotations.[15]

For almost two millenia, then, Christians have been deriving, invalidly, hatred of Jews from the gospel of love, a situation clearly intolerable today in the light of the Holocaust. Yet, just as clearly, we as Church have no right to change or amend the sacred texts themselves. "Obviously", the Vatican Guidelines remind us, "one cannot alter the text of the Bible." Yet the same passage in the Guidelines, addressed to "commissions entrusted with the task of liturgical translation" goes on to advise that in translating the Bible for liturgical use "there should be an overriding preoccupation to bring out explicitly the meaning of a text while taking Scriptual studies into account", and suggests as an example that 'Ioudaioi' be translated differently depending on its actual meaning in a given passage.

In a recent discussion of the meaning of the New Testament term 'Ioudaioi' Malcolm Lowe argues that the usual translation of the term as "The Jews" is, on strict critical grounds, both inconsistent and erroneous. He concludes his study with a plea for a more accurate translation:

> There is already a need to amend the current mistranslations in the gospels, since rendering of 'Ioudaioi' "the Jews" is not only incorrect (and inconsistent with rendering 'Ioudaia' as "Judea") but also pernicious. As long as the mistranslation continues, generations will continue to read that "the Jews" had Jesus killed and (by combining this with Mt. 27:25) to infer that they declared themselves and their descendants responsible. Thus this philological error (a confusion of the Palestinian use of Ioudaios to distinguish Judeans from Galileans, etc., with its wider meanings in the Diaspora) has provided, in practically all modern translations of the gospels, a constant excuse for antisemitism whose further existence cannot be permitted.[16]

It is interesting to note that the Good News New Testament put out by the American Bible Society (Fourth Edition) does attempt to reflect such scholarship, quite successfully in many passages.

Dr. Raymond Brown, whose Johannine research for the Anchor Bible, and in his more recent The Community of the Beloved Disciple has analyzed the multiple polemics, internal and

external, reflected in the Fourth Gospel, would seem to oppose
such an approach:

> In the evolution of the term it is helpful to note
> that John can refer interchangeably to "the Jews" and
> to the chief priests and Pharisees . . . But this
> interchangeability is not to be interpreted benevo-
> lently as it is by those who wish to remove the term
> "the Jews" from the Fourth Gospel by substituting
> "Jewish authorities" or worse still... "Judeans"...
> John deliberately uses the same term for the Jewish
> authorities of Jesus' time and for the hostile
> inhabitants of the synagogue of his own time... It
> would be incredible for a twentieth-century Christian
> to share or justify the Johannine contention that
> "the Jews" are the children of the devil, an
> affirmation that is placed on the lips of Jesus
> (8:44); but I cannot see how it helps contemporary
> Jewish-Christian relationships to disguise the fact
> that such an attitude once existed.[17]

In Bible editions designed for study or private reading
where notations and commentaries can make clear the historical
contingencies involved, I would agree wholeheartedly with
Father Brown. Versions destined for liturgical use, however
represent a different situation, as the Vatican Guidelines
recognize. We are not facing in our congregations a tabula
raza, where our people accept God's Word in isolated, academic
neutrality and have time to discuss the issues. The context
is a sacred one, charged with immediacy of impact. And our
congregations have been carefully prepared, with a catechesis
stretching back for centuries, to view Jews "in an unfavorable
light."

The liturgy, in its selection and disposition of texts,
imposes an interpretation. Hence, within the range of
allowable linguistic variants, an "overriding preoccupation"
may justify translations which would appear strained in other
contexts. We already, for example, use modern equivalents for
denominations of ancient currency, or other paraphrases to
facilitate the communicability or drama of various pericopes.
A second option also presents itself. In the Catholic
liturgical tradition, it is quite common to omit verses or
whole sections to serve the point of the liturgical theme or
simply to promote piety. The prudent use of such discretional
options might help greatly to reduce the likelihood of misunderstanding, without "altering" the text. Passages such as
"Susanah and the Elders", for example, are already optional at
the discretion of the celebrant because they might be pis
auribus offensivus (offensive to pious ears). The present
lectionary contains numerous deletions and elisions from the
Scriptural text, especially in the first readings and the
responsorial psalms, usually for the sake of brevity, but also

for reasons of piety. The first reading for the Seventh Sunday of the year (82c), for example, is from 1 Samuel 26, verses 2, 7-9; 12-13, 22-23. Omitted are references to David "hiding on the hill" (v.1), seemingly hoping that god will take care of Saul for him (v. 10), and rather nastily taunting both Abner and Saul (14-21). If such relatively innocuous passages as these can be omitted for fear of giving offense by making a biblical hero "look bad" one must ask, how much more so (qal va homer) in the case of established anti-Judaic passages?

Application of such traditional liturgical principles to the present situation, then, at the very least would open a valid avenue of exploration, whatever the ultimate conclusions reached. The three readings from Matthew 23:13-22 now used in the Lectionary, for example, could easily be replaced with units taken from Matthew 24:1-35, which is not currently used in the Proper of the Season, but only on the feast day of June 30. This would not even interrupt the natural flow of the cycle. Matthew 27:25 ("His blood be upon us...") could also be dropped without endangering the central impact of the passion narrative. In short, a creative approach, following quite traditional liturgical practice in such matters, could combine various options to greatly alleviate the present dilemma, although much study is still necessary because of the complexity of the questions raised.

But even if this is accomplished, a tremendous educational effort is demanded today. Christians must learn to read and hear the Bible in its historical context, and to take that context into account when interpreting it either communally or in private study. Matthew's attack on the Pharisees reflect his own times, not Jesus', and this basic fact must ever be borne in mind, John, not Jesus tends to lump the Jews together into a single, stereotypical ball.

This I see, as the only way out of a very real dilemma facing us. History has shown that the Scriptures, read indiscriminately and through the polemic "filters" of patristic theology, can promote hatred rather than love from our pulpits. In introducing a recent collection of twelve major essays responding to this precise challenge, among others, raised by Rosemary Reuther's trenchant, if inconclusive work, Faith and Fraticide,[18] Alan T. Davies comments:

> If a common motif in these essays can be described, it is the conviction that Christians need not choose between an ideological defense of their scriptures that wards off damaging criticism and the sad conclusion that the New Testament is so wholly contaminated by anti-Jewish prejudice as to lose all moral authority. Instead, through careful study, Christians can isolate what genuine forms of anti-

Judaism really color the major writings, and, by examining their historic genesis, neutralize their potential for harm.[19]

Positive Ambiguities

While the corrective goal thus seems at least achievable if we can continue the present momentum with renewed commitment, the positive goal is much more difficult and fraught with ambiguities. While there is a general consensus about the negative images of Jews and Judaism that need to be eliminated or placed in their contingent, historical context in our catechesis, no such clear consensus, I believe, yet exists on how we should refashion our Christian understanding of Judaism to achieve a positive theological appreciation of its ongoing validity without seeming to "back down" from our own central, creedal claims.

My own study of textbooks, for example, found the category dealing with "the relationship between the covenants" the only one to contain a preponderance of ambiguous statements.[20] This failure of the educators to come up with a clear vision, however, needs to be understood as a reflection of the fact that this remains an unanswered set of questions even among the best of our theologians. Michael B. McGarry's Christology after Auschwitz[21] and the more recent Antisemitism and the Foundations of Christianity[22] illustrate the efforts in this direction. To succeed, the effort needs to include a much wider group of Christian thinkers - especially our major systematicians - than have heretofore taken up this complex and sensitive challenge. Part of the dilemma for the scholars so far involved in the debate is, as James Parkes phrases it, whether "the basic root of modern anti-semitism lies squarely on the Gospels and the rest of the New Testament."[23] For several reasons, however, I believe this framing of the question to be something of a red-herring.[24] The negative theological roots for what was to blossom as Christian anti-semitism (fully formed only some centuries later) can surely be culled from the pages of the New Testament. But different and more positive seeds, such as those in Romans 9-11,[25] can be found there as well. The exigencies of subsequent history, not any absolute theological necessities, I would maintain, are where we must search for the whys and hows of the development of Christian anti-semitism from its apostolic-period beginnings. Chrysostum, after all, was precipitated into his fanatical diatribes against the Jews not by his theological studies but by the simpler fact that many of his congregants preferred Jewish services and preaching to his own. And if there was any inevitability about the process, as Professor Yosef Yerushalmi has pointed out, genocide against the Jews would have occurred during the Middle Ages when Christendom had absolute power over the Jews of Europe and not in the modern era when the political power of the Churches had long been broken and dispersed.[26]   This, of course, does not let Christians off the hook.   For it can equally be said that without the traditional Christian teaching of contempt the Jews could never have been so easily scapegoated by Nazism. Had Christianity not so tragically laid the ground with its earlier teachings, Auschwitz might never have occurred.

Be this as it may, the heart of the current theological debate, I believe, is over what will replace the old polemic. Almost all of the theologians that I know of who have taken up the question in a systematic way to date, seem to agree that any resolution of the problem will involve more or less signi- ficant adjustments in fundamental areas of Christian theology such as ecclesiology, Christology, and eschatology.

Here I would like to suggest that the common-sense insight which Davies prescribes for the "antisemitism in the New Testament" debate can equally be applied in the present, less tractable instance.   We can, with integrity and delicacy, adjust our understanding of certain Christian themes without in any real way endangering or "watering down" core Christian beliefs, and still I believe, end the triumphalism of the past.   Indeed, such a careful surgical process will actually result in a more authentic holding of our traditions, one cleansed as it were of the barnacles of contempt which have so often in the past obscurred the essence of our faith, even from ourselves.[27]

Monica Hellwig, Gregory Baum and John T. Pawlikowski all argue strongly from a Catholic point of view for such a possi- bility, though they articulate their own alternatives in dif- fering (but not necessarily incompatible) ways.[28]

Here I would like to explore this possibility with reference to a single issue, one which has profound implica- tions both for the structure of our liturgy and the basic style of our proclamation of the Word in our liturgy.   This is the promise-fulfillment theme.

Promise and Fulfillment

The reason I center on this particular theme, rooted as it is so deeply in the New Testament and in the liturgy, is not simply the structure of this conference and the topic of preaching assigned to me.   Rather, it is a theme which I believe is central to the whole endeavor outlined above, but which has recieved distressingly little attention as such in the discussion to date, especially among liturgists.

It is, however, integral to the issues raised by Parkes, Reuther and others and, with the concreteness of its application for the present structure of the selection of liturgical readings, capable (if resolved) both of implementation in a reasonable way and of serving as a paradigm for approaching other, related aspects of the overall quest for an adequate Christian theology of Judaism. What the endeavor requires for success, I will argue, is not some full-scale rooting out of central Christian beliefs, but merely the re-capturing of that humility of spirit urged on us by St. Paul in his image of the root and branch, however that image is exegetically construed: "remember that you do not support the root; the root supports you."[29]

The promise-fulfillment theme, in varying measures, lies at the heart of the approach to the Hebrew Scriptures employed by the New Testament authors.[30] The theme is equally important for understanding the rationale behind the choice of passages from the Hebrew Scriptures included in the current lectionary. While not critical (if subtly ever-present) in the selections for much of the liturgical cycle, its use is obvious and clear in the Lenten and Advent readings, with their reliance on the major prophets (especially Isaiah and Jeremiah).

The present application of this theme, however, can and should be critiqued sensitively from the point of view of Jewish-Christian relations. While I am not at all arguing for its abandonment, I do maintain that some careful re-thinking of the whole question needs to be done today in the light of modern scholarship.

Father John L. McKenzie, S. J., for example, does no more than articulate a growing consensus among biblical scholars when he states that:

> This writer has said elsewhere that Jesus is the Messiah of Judaism, and that he can be understood only as Messiah of Judaism. I stand by this observation, but I do not believe that it obliges me to find faith in Jesus Messiah in the Old Testament [Sic] , nor to base faith in Jesus Messiah in the Old Testament. Jesus transformed the idea of Messiah when he fulfilled it. The total reality of Jesus Messiah is found nowhere in the Old Testament, not even in its totality. Jesus would have emerged from nothing except Israel and the Old Testament; but the study of the Old Testament does not demand that Jesus Messiah emerge from it.[31]

Now this is striking, and indeed a radical statement. It is even more striking when one considers that it comes, not from the pen of one who wishes to further the Jewish-Christian dialogue, but one who is simply and straightforwardly interested in objectively summarizing the theological thrusts of the Hebrew Scriptures on their own terms.

Perhaps the phrase "on their own terms" pinpoints best the difference between McKenzie and previous generations of scholars.[32] And it is a phrase which summarizes as well the whole enterprise, from the Christian side, of the current dialogue. Can Christianity, in essence, understand and accept Judaism as a salvific reality on its own terms? Or does the Christian selfdefinition inherently necessitate a view of Israel which subordinates its role in the divine plan to that of the Church?

The Vatican Guidelines referred to above seem to call us to at least make an attempt at achieving the first option:

> Christians must therefore strive to acquire a better knowledge of the basic components of the religious traditions of Judaism; they must strive to learn by what essential traits the Jews define themselves in the light of their own religious tradition.[33]

Beginning with the New Testament period itself, one might add, Christians have used a range of approaches to avoid directly encountering the questions embedded in its reliance on the promise-fulfillment theme as a key hermeneutical tool for interpreting the Hebrew Bible accepted by Jesus and the Apostles as God's word.

Christians, I would submit, have always been aware (if grudgingly) that the first coming of Jesus did not see the fulfillment of the biblical promises as God gave them or as the Jews (in their diverse but interrelated ways)[34] understood them. Thus we see already in Paul the beginnings of the two major interpretational devices Christianity was to utilize to explain how Jesus could be Messiah without there being a Messianic Age in evidence. These were typology and allegory. In Romans 5:14, for example, Adam is called "a type of the one to come," and Paul maintains that Adam corresponds to Christ not only in resemblance, but also by difference (see also Cor. 15). In Galatians, Paul, in a way reminiscent of Philo before him, consciously allegorizes Genesis 16:15 as a foreshadowing of his own theology of spiritual slavery and freedom (Galatians 4:22-26).

But typology and allegory are used throughout the New Testament as ways for illuminating the "real" meaning of passages in the Hebrew Scriptures as referring to Jesus for their fulfillment, sometimes in conformity with and at other times almost in direct opposition to the original intent of the Hebrew biblical passages in their own historical context. The Apostolic authors' uses of allegory and typology serve the purpose of stressing the continuity between God's relations with the Jews as a Chosen People and the revelation that comes in and through Jesus.

But such frames for an admittedly paradoxical relationship are, as subsequent Christian history has shown, all too easily capable of abuse. Already in the second century, Marcion of Pontus, stressing the discontinuous pole of the relationship, sought to abandon the Hebrew Bible altogether (and, incidentally, much of the New Testament as well, considering it too "Jewish" to meet with the approval of the sophisticated Greek and Roman audiences he sought to convert.) Wisely, Marcion's doctrine was condemned, although many of his stereotypes, particularly the dichotomy between the Torah of fear and justice and the gospel of love and mercy, etc., became standard fare in Christian preaching despite the heterodoxy of their underlying rationale.

And the New Testament stress on continuity all too easily came to be used to undergird the patristic theory of supercession, in which everything "good" about Judaism was viewed as "really" Christian and subsumed into Christianity. Thus, essential Jewish insights, such as the covenant of love of Deuteronomy 6 and Jeremiah were turned back on their own authors to "prove" the superiority of Christianity.

Continuity and discontinuity in the promises, however, are the poles in a dynamic tension found within the New Testament, both of which must be carefully preserved in tension if our own self-articulation as Christians is not to reduce itself to a mere set of fanciful theories lacking any contact with the realities of the human condition. Father David Tracy recently devoted a major paper to recapturing this sense of tension between the "already here" of "realized" eschatology and the "not yet" which must accompany it.[35] The latter, of course, is the humble admission that for all of our sophisticated theology, we must recognize that the Jews in respect of the promises make a basically valid point: the Messianic Age is not here. Neither universal peace nor universal justice, its central "signs", today reign over the earth as God has promised they will. For Christians to claim that Jesus is divine is one thing, and quite valid. Even to claim that Jesus is Messiah, as McKenzie does, can be valid. But to make such a claim without at the same time admitting that the Kingdom of God is still in process is crass triumphalism.

Douglas John Hallin his contribution the collection edited by Alan Davies referred to above comments from a Protestant point of view that "it is hardly possible to hear the whole testimony of the New Testament to the 'new reality' in Christ, without sensing the presence of a strong critique of any confusion of Church and Kingdom."[36] Hall goes on to apply Tillich's designation of "The Protestant Principle" to the

present question: "nothing conditional may assume the posture
of the unconditional."[37]   By equating the Church, whose
mission is precisely to build the Kingdom, with the Kingdom
itself, we allow the basic New Testament tension between the
"already here" and the "not yet" to dissipate.

Applications for Christian Preaching Today

Many   of   the   more   recent   versions   of   the   promise-
fulfillment theme, which comes to us under the guise of the
"objective" and "scientific" results of late 19th Century
biblical scholarship equally need to be criticized before we
continue   to   proclaim   them   from   the   pulpit.   The
"Heilsgeschichte" or "salvation history" approach is one
such.[38]

This theory owes much of its popularity to Wellhausen.
Like the dichotomies of Marcion it is both simple and dramatic, which has made it particularly alluring to preachers and
teachers alike.   Wellhausen's vision relies heavily on an
adaptation of Social Darwinism, with it its "later is better"
motif, and on the use of the Hegelian dialectic as a philo-
sophical "filter" for organizing all of the biblical material
in a single, grand scheme.   The fact that the biblical revelation refuses to be encapsulated adequately into such a pre-
programmed procrustean bed did not deter Wellhausen, who
simply ignored anything that didn't "fit".

Briefly, Wellhausen finds the initial stage (thesis) of
the development in the "purity" of the Patrical Age and the
desert experience of the Exodus.   This pure monotheism is,
however, corrupted by the obscurantist legalism of the priests
(antithesis), necessitating the rise of the prophets to return
Israel to the purity of ethical monotheism (synthesis).   This
new thesis is in turn clouded by the legalism of the Pharisees
(new antithesis) necessitating Jesus' condemnation of them and
the establishment of a new synthesis (Christianity) to replace
the now moribund and discardable Judaism.

Aside from the fact that Wellhausen's theory is a thinly-
veiled attack on Roman Catholicism (with its priesthood and
canon law), it fails in the basic test of history.   Judaism
refused to stay dead.   The Jews have continued in faithful
adherence to God's covenant and in developing a rich religious
tradition after Jesus right up to the present.   As McKenzie
comments:

It   is   time   today   to   say   goodbye   to
Heilsgeschichte. As a principle of unity of biblical
theology, the history of salvation is as contrived
and strained as any dialectic ever invented.   It

assumes that the New Testament is a term toward which everything in the Old Testament was directed. Elements of the Old Testament in which this direction cannot be seen must be twisted to fit the scheme or omitted from the history of salvation.[39]

The first direct application of both modern biblical scholarship and of the fruits of the dialogue as I have enunciated them above, then, lies in the rigorous critique each one of us must make of our own patterns of preaching. To what extent do we abuse what is valid in the promise-fulfillment theme by absolutizing it and ignoring the creative tension between "what is" and "what ought to be" that is its major lesson for Christians today? To what extent do we follow the easy path of dichotomies or simplistic theories like Wellhausen's as a filter between our hearers and the Word of God in its full, pregnant majesty?

The second application lies in a systematic critique of the structure of our liturgical readings themselves. To what extent have we chosen readings from the Hebrew Scriptures based solely on a simplistic understanding of the promise-fulfillment theme? Are we being true, in our liturgy, to the fullness of the biblical revelation of the Hebrew Scriptures if we allow this single theme, however important, to serve as the sole guiding light in determining which selections of readings we take from the Hebrew Bible to highlight in our Sunday and weekday cycles?

The Hebrew Scriptures are capable of challenging Christians on many levels. Our liturgy, to the extent of our ability, should reflect their widest range and depth rather than allowing itself to become fixated on a single hermeneutical principle, especially one which has seen such abuse in the past.

Implications for Theology

Further, I believe that such a reexamination of liturgical readings, and of the principles that underly their selection, can help to illuminate the pressing questions involved in the theological reassessment of the relationship between the convenants alluded to above (and be aided in turn by it). For when looked at from this perspective, it begins to be clear that the "adjustments" required in Christian theology, if we are to attain our goal of a prejudice free proclamation of the good news, may not be so severely "radical" as many of us have feared. Rather, what we are about is the clarification and reauthentication of our vision, freeing it from centuries of association with a polemic against Judaism we can now see was

never necessary to it from the start (though we convinced ourselves it was).

Christ is God.   This we can state without ambiguity.
Though we thereby enunciate a disagreement with the Jewish
community, it is not a disagreement which inevitably must lead
us beyond difference to a theological collision course.
Equally, we affirm that Christ is man and as man is Jewish.
As Christians, we can, and must, admit with Vatican II the
continuing validity of Judaism on its own terms for its own
people.   God, as Nostra Aetate declares, "does not repent of
the gifts He makes nor of the calls that He issues" (see
Romans 9-11).

In one sense, we continue to proclaim that Jesus is the
Messiah.   The Good News is that God, in becoming incarnate in
Jesus, definitively reveals His involvement in and solidarity
with human suffering.[40] But, humbly, we must also acknowledge
what this definitive "saving deed" of God does not mean, that
is, what remains to be done.   It does not mean that the
Parousia is here, or that the Messianic Age has been achieved.
In Jesus, we have a foretaste, a security, even a surety of
hope.   But we have only the first step.   We admit that the
full eschatological event has not been handed us magically on
a silver platter.   We remain within history with all of its
ambiguities.   The "already here" is constantly balanced with
the instantly uttered "not yet" as in the New Testament
itself.   Stripped of arrogance, we can begin, together with
the Jewish people, to whose divinely gifted covenant our own
is in the Jew Jesus engrafted, to build that Kingdom.

Judaism has no claims, one way or another, about
Christology (its "no" being not so much active as passive).
It does have claims concerning the nature of the Messianic
Age.   It is these which we must heed, to be true to ourselves.

The crunch between our communities, then, is not so much
Christological as it is eschatological.   The questions raised
by dialogue are not those of the essential nature of Jesus as
human and divine but of the historical and eschatological
implications of the Christ-event.

Eschatology and the Virtue of Humility

Here I find that I agree with much of what is positive in
Rosemary Reuther's book, though I would dissent from much that
is absolutist or needlessly harsh in her phrasings.   Her
cautions against "spiritualizing the eschatological" and
against "historicizing the eschatological" are particularly
apt.   And being central to her thesis[41] they also show that

even for her the problem is primarily in the realm of eschatology rather than Christology as such - however closely linked
the two are viewed in our academic flow-chart of the divisions
of theology as a field of study.

By "spiritualizing the eschatological", Reuther means the
tendency to state, falsely, that the Messianic Age is "already
here", without uttering the immediate "not yet" which gave the
claim reality. To justify this assertion we declare that the
Messianic Promises should be understood to refer to the realm
of the "spiritual". Here we assume that the proclamation "we
are saved", means "our souls are saved" rather than that
history itself is truly affected by the Christ-event. This,
as we have seen, can lead to the path of false allegorization
of the biblical message.

Reuther's   second   caution,   against   "historizing   the
eschatological", is equally salutatory. This pinpoints the
tendency to equate what is promised (the Messianic Age) with
some institution in history (normally the Church), ascribing
to that contingent, human institution a form of perfection
that can only be longed for in this life. This leads to the
way of false triumphalism.

The 1974 Vatican Guidelines, in a passage little referred
to but quite pertinent here, provides one way of stating well
all that I have been trying to say. Interestingly it is in
the section concerning the liturgy and directed specifically
to liturgists and homilists. Cautiously worded, it constitutes a highly significant admission in the true spirit of
humility:

> When commenting on Biblical texts, emphasis will be
> laid on the continuity of our faith with that of the
> earlier covenant in the perspective of the promises,
> without minimizing these elements of Christianity
> which are original! We believe that those promises
> were fulfilled with the first coming of Christ. But
> it is nonetheless true that we still await their <u>per-
> fect</u> <u>fulfillment</u> in His glorious return at the end of
> time.

A distinction such as this between "fulfilled" and
"perfectly fulfilled", perhaps, only makes sense within the
context of that uniquely diplomatic form of theological
discourse that I would privately label "Vaticanese". It does
not resolve all of the theological "mysteries" (understanding
that term in its precise sense) raised by Jewish-Christian
relations.   Nor does it diminish the seriousness and
complexity of the task that lies ahead for Christians. As Dr.
Paul van Buren said, addressing the Christian side of a
Jewish-Christian dialogue:

To invite you into a theological acknowledgement, or theological affirmation of the Jews and Judaism, is to invite you into a project touching every aspect of our existence together as the Church of Jesus Christ. To take up this project as to take on every aspect of our life and thought as Christians.[42]

But it does help us to focus on the real issues, thereby limiting our natural tendencies as theologians to flights of rhetorical fancy. The urgency of the issue, however defined, remains, as well as the burning shame we should feel as Christians for not having taken it up long ago.

NOTES

[1]The distinction is an important one to make. The content and
practical consequences of such a basic Christian term as
"witness", for example, varies widely from one Christian denomination to another. For many Catholics "witness" connotes
primarily social action and charity, love evinced by word and
deed (up to and including martyrdom). For many Protestants,
"witness" can mean primarily active missionizing, proselytism.
Hence a distinction such as that made by Professor Tommaso
Federici in his now famous study, "The Mission and Witness of
the Church", (Origins, Oct. 19, 1978, 273-283) between witness
and proselytism of the Jews would result in quite diverse
forms of behavior toward Jews in these communities.

[2]For a precise and complete definition of this term, see Jules
Issac, The Teaching of Contempt: Christian Roots of Anti-
-Semitism (New York: Holt, Rinehart, Winston, 1971). For a
survey-description of the results of this teaching see Edward
H. Flannery, The Anguish of the Jews (N.Y.: Macmillan, 1965).

[3]A. Roy Eckardt, Your People, My People (N.Y.: Quadrangle,
1974) p. 79.

[4]Vatican Commission for Religious Relations with the Jews,
"Guidelines and Suggestions for Implementing the Conciliar
Declaration Nostra Aetate, (no. 4)", December 1, 1974. The
rest of this same paragraph is also of interest here, since it
amounts to a frank admission that the Catholic Church needs
the dialogue with both Judaism and other Christian Churches as
a part of its own vital process of self-definition:
"Therefore, even in areas where no Jewish communities exist,
this remains an important problem. There is also an ecumenical aspect to the question. The very return of Christians to
the sources and origins of their faith, grafted on to the
earlier Covenant, helps the search for unity in Christ, the
cornerstone."

[5]This should begin to make clear my own position on the issue
of whether and to what extent anti-semitism can be said to be
present in the New Testament itself. Some scholars, such as
Rosemary Reuther and Gregory Baum, are inclined to the posi-
tion that the New Testament polemics against Judaism (e.g.,
Matthew's invective against the Pharisees or Paul against "The
Law") are more or less inherently anti-semitic. (See R.
Reuther, Faith and Fratricide, N.Y.: Seabury, 1974, with
Baum's introduction). Others such as Edward Flannery (The
Anguish of the Jews, N. Y.: Macmillan, 1965) argue that true
Christian antisemitism begins only with the Fathers of the

Church. What went before is an internal family struggle. The bitterness of certain New Testament passages is explained by the very closeness of the two related groups. While Samuel Sandmel's Antisemitism in the New Testament? (Phila.: Fortress, 1978) uses the term "antisemitism throughout, its thrust appears actually closer to Flannery than Reuther. The real argument, as we shall see below, is not whether there exists an anti-Judaic polemic in the New Testament; there certainly does. The question is whether this polemic is an essential element of the New Testament message or simply a reflection of the historical contingencies surrounding the apostolic writings.

[6]Eugene Fisher, "A Content Analysis of the Treatment of Jews and Judaism in Current Roman Catholic Textbooks and Manuals on the Primary and Secondary Levels", Ph.D. Dissertation, New York University, 1976. See also, Eugene Fisher, Faith Without Prejudice: Rebuilding Christian Attitudes Toward Judaism (N.Y.: Paulist, 1977 hereafter); "Furthering The Jewish-Christian Dialogue", Professional Approaches for Christian Educators (PACE, Vol. 7, 1976, Teaching A").

[7]These studies took the form of three unpublished doctoral dissertations, for St. Louis University; Sr. Rita Mudd, F.S.C.P., "Intergroup Relations in Social Studies Curriculum" (1961); Sr. M. Linus Gleason, C.S.J., "Intergroup Relations as Revealed by Content Analysis of Literature Textbooks Used in Catholic Secondary Schools" (1958); Sr. Rose Thering, O.P., "Potential in Religious Textbooks for Developing a Realistic Self-Concept" (1961). It is significant that aside from a brief progress report issued by Maher for the Journal of the Religious Education Association (Vol LV, No.2, 133-138), the results of these studies were not published until over a decade later by John T. Pawlikowski, O.S.M Catechetics and Prejudice: How Catholic Teaching Materials View Jews, Protestant and Racial Minorities (N.Y. Paulist, 1973). Pawlikowski notes that "here we have a reflection of the mind-set of the pre-Vatican II Church". (p. 10)

[8]An excellent selection of both Catholic and Protestant documents can be found in Helga Croner, editor, Stepping Stones to Further Jewish-Christian Relations (London: Stimulus, 1977).

[9]Vatican Guidelines, cf. footnote 4.

[10]John T. Townsend's A Liturgical Interpretation of Our Lord's Passion in Narrative Form, "Israel Study Group Occasional Papers, No. 1" (N.Y.: NCCJ, 1977) provides excellent aid to the homilist and liturgist in coping with the Passion Narratives.

[11]A wide range of Materials already exists to assist the preacher in this task. Krister Stendahl's Holy Week in the

"Proclamation: Aids for Interpreting the Lessons of the Church Year" Phila.: Fortress, 1974); Gerard S. Slyan, Commentary on the New Lectionary (N.Y.: Paulist, 1975); and my own suggested "Guidelines" for Catechists and Homilists" (both available from the Secretariat for Catholic-Jewish Relations, 1312 Massachusetts Ave., N.W., Washington, D.C. 20005) come to mind. Excellent materials have also been produced on the local level. The Archdiocese of Los Angeles, for example, has issued "Lenten Pastoral Reflections", which are short comments "to be included in the bulletin and to be read prior to the first reading at Sunday Liturgies during Lent". These cover cycles A, B, and C. Finally the diocese of Memphis has put out an Commentary on the Gospel of Matthew (N.Y.: Paulist, 1978) as well as a brief "Background" pamphlet on the Lenten materials. A brief bibliography of majorworks on the trial of Jesus can be found in my FWP, cit., 172-4. 11aSee FWP, cit., 42-46; 66-72.

[12]FWP, cit, 33-35; 62-75; 81-86 and bibliography. See also Sandmel, op. cit.

[13]E. g., Earl Richard, "The Polemical Character of the Joseph Episode in Acts 7," JBL 19/2 (1975) 255-67. Where scholars as recent as Martin Dibelius in 1956 still argued that Acts 7:9-16 was a "neutral history", Richard convincingly shows that an anti-Jewish polemic marks the whole of the speech: "Far from being straightforward history, Acts 7: is as violently polemic as are vv 51-53 of the speech...The same is not true of the Joseph episode of Gen. 37-50." (p.259).

[14]For a convenient summary of the literature and bibliography see Urban C. von Wahlde, "The Terms for Religious Authorities in the Fourth Gospel," JBL 98/2 (1979) 231-53.

[15]Ibid., 234.

[16]M. Lowe, "Who Were the Ioudaioi?", Novum Testamentum, Vol XVIII: 101-130, p. 130.

[17]Raymon E. Brown, S.S., The Community of the Beloved Disciple (N.Y.: Paulist, 1979), 41-42.

[18]Rosemary Radford Reuther, Faith and Fratricide: The Theological Roots of Anti-Semitism (N.Y.: Seabury, 1974).

[19]Alan T. Davies, editor, Antisemitism and the Foundations Christianity (N.Y.: Paulist, 1979).

[20]FWP, 130-139. The chapter dealing with this issue is likewise tentative and descriptive of the various options rather than conclusive (FWP, 89-97).
[21]Michael B. McGarry, Christology After Auschwitz (N.Y.: Paulist, 1977).

[22]Alan T. Davies, op., cit. John T. Pawlikowski, OSM, provides an excellent overview of the current state of the debate in his article, "Christ and the Jewish-Christian Dialogue" (Chicago Studies, Fall, 1977, 367-389).

[23]Preface to Antisemitism and the Foundations of Christianity, op. cit., xi.

[24]See footnote 5 above.

[25]See "Statement on Catholic-Jewish Relations", National Conference of Catholic Bishops, Nov. 20, 1975.

[26]Yosef Hayim Yerushalmi, "Response to Rosemary Reuther," in Eva Fleischner, ed., Auschwitz: Beginning of a New Era? (N.Y.: KTAV, Cathedral, ADL, 1977) 97-107.

[27]An example on the negative side can be found in the ancient deicide canard. Since Christianity, as its heart, proclaims the good news that Jesus comes to save all humanity from sin, our core belief ., that it is sin that must be held responsible for his death.

Unless we as Christians accept our responsibility (blame, guilt) for Jesus' death, we cannot, in the Pauline vision, participate in the hope of his resurrection. The deicide charge, by projecting blame for the Crucifixion away from the true conspirators (all of us in our common sinfulness) externalized the Paschal mystery and thus deprived it of any real meaning in our own lives as Christians. In blaming Jews for Jesus' death, we Christians effectively seal ourselves off from our own vision of salvation.

[28]Davies, op., cit., 118-166.

[29]Romans 11:18 (NAE). Pauline studies in the past few years have been undergoing a virtual revolution as the result of the fruits of the Christian-Jewish dialogue. Among others, one could cite as evidence Krister Stendahl's Paul Among Jews and Gentiles (Phila: Fortress, 1976); H.J. Schoeps, Paul: The Theology of the Apostle in the Light of Jewish Religious History, translated by H. Knight (Lutterworth Press, 1961; Phila: Westminster edition, 1979); Gerard Sloyan, Is Christ the End of the Law and E.P. Sanders; magnificent Paul and Palestinian Judaism (Phila.: Fortress, 1977).

[30]E.g., see Henry M. Shires' handy Compilation Finding the Old Testament in the New (Phila.: Westminster, 1974), esp. 31-64. See my earlier article on "Continuity and Discontinuity in the Scriptural Readings," Liturgy (May, 1978) 30-37 where I argue that "...the power of Advent and Easter would be impoverished...without the use of typology or fulfillment

themes in the liturgy." (p. 32)

[31]John L. McKenzie, S.J., A Theology of the Old Testament (N.Y.: Doubleday Image, 1976) 31-32.

[32]Such as Rudolf Bultmann, who argued vociferously that the sole function of the Hebrew Scriptures for the Christian was as a mere propadeutic for the New Testament, thus reducing the immediacy of divine revelation in the former to a set of useful but by no means critical background papers for the latter. See Bultmann's article, and the rejoinder essays in Bernard W. Anderson, editor, The Old Testament and Christian Faith (N.Y.,: Herder Herder, 1969).

[33]Cited in FWP, 152.

[34]For an understanding of some of the many messianic understandings current in New Testament times, see Samson H. Levey, The Messiah: An Aramaic Interpretation. The Messianic Exegisis of the Targum (Cincinnati: HUC/JIR, 1974), "Monographs of the Hebrew Union College, No. II."

[35]Rev. David Tracy, "The Dialogue between Jewish and Christian Theologies: Some Reflections", paper delivered at Washington Theological Union Coalition Seminar on the topic, March 9, 1979, Washington, D.C.

[36]Hall, "Rethinking Christ", in Davies, op. cit., 172.

[37]Ibid., 185.

[38]I have summarized several other popular versions in my Liturgy article (see footnote 23, above. German theological products, both exegetical and systematic, need to be used with caution today. See the strong critiques of them in Eva Fleischner, The View of Judaism in German Theology since 1945 (Milwaukee: Marquette Univ., Ph.D. Thesis, 1971); Charlotte Klein, Anti-Judaism in Christian Theology (Phila.: Fortress, 1978); E.P. Sanders, op. cit., "From Polemic to Objectivity: The Use and Abuse of Hebrew Sources in Christian New Testament Scholarship", a paper delivered at the Annual meeting of the AAR/SBL, Nov. 20, 1979, E. Fisher.

[39]McKenzie, op., cit., 341.

[40]Application of this insight to the Holocaust, of course, remains a vital task of our major theologians today.

[41]As John T. Pawlikowski rightly points out in his "Historicizing the Eschatological; Spiritualizing the Eschatological: Some Reflections", in Davies, op. cit., 151-166.

[42]Rev. Paul van Buren, "Toward Theological Acknowledgment of the Jews", a paper delivered at General Theological Seminary, New York City, Nov. 10, 1976.

Chapter Four

THE JEWISH PEOPLE IN CHRISTIAN PREACHING: A PROTESTANT

PERSPECTIVE

Krister Stendahl

I

We turn to the subject of preaching because that is where
it all is supposed to come together. I think we have now been
sufficiently and rightly informed that the Christian Bible has
a lot of ugly things on its conscience. I think it is very
important to face that fact squarely. The usual gimmick is to
say: "Of course the Bible is 'kosher'; there cannot be any
bad things in the Bible. When things went wrong it was always
the bad Christians who fall short of the high standards of the
Bible." I never liked that argument. It's a little like
Chesterton's statement, "They say that Christianity has
failed. I rather suggest it has not been tried yet." That is
cute, and very clever, and quite untrue, for I think 2,000
years is a reasonable testing period. And it is obvious that
in this atomic power station called "the scriptures," there
are enormous risks for harmful radiation fallout. To be a
preacher, as well as a theologian is to learn to counteract
the fallout and bring the power that is, toward peaceful and
beneficial use. That is an important part of the task of
preaching.

I am a Lutheran, and Luther had his bad days and his good
days, not the least in relation to Jewish-Christian questions.
But on one of his good days, he almost quoted Michael Cook by
saying that the word of God is not the word of the Bible but
the preached word, i.e. that ongoing living tradition of
interpretation which Michael Cook spoke of as underdeveloped
in the Christian tradition.

To be a preacher is to be guided right in interpreting and
applying the Word. One of the ways in which we can learn to
do this better, knowing the gruesome history of Biblical anti-
Semitism, is to think about the words of Jesus according to

the Gospel of Matthew in the Sermon on the Mount. In a kind of Yom Kippur setting Jesus says: "So, if you are offering your gift at the altar and then remember that your brother (or sister) has something against you, leave your gift there before the altar and go first and be reconciled to your brother (or sister), and then come and offer your gift" (Mt. 5:23-24). Most Christians, when they hear that word, hear it as if it said: "When you come to the altar and you remember that you have something against your brother or your sister, lay down your gift..." What is the difference? The difference is momentous. Jesus said, 'and you remember that the other one has something against you'. That's the only important thing. Your own feelings you will always read as relatively good. "Some of our best friends are Jews." Of course, we love everybody. We are all people of good will, not only at Christmas time. The unmasking can only happen when you start to wonder if, for some reason, the other has something against you.

And there is only one way in which Christians can find that out, and blessed are we in these United States because we can use that way. We can go to the rabbi of our choice in the community and ask how that which we preach sounds to him. That's the only way. We Christians have no Jewish ears. There is no way in which we can hear. So that is the first rule about Judaism in Christian preaching. Because to preach means to be responsible not for what one says, not even for what we think we say, but for what we are heard to say. That is why preaching is so tough. Scholars who write books, if misunderstood, can always answer the review that attacked them in one way or another and the discussion goes on and on. But somehow, once the word is thrown out from the pulpit, there are no controls. The tragedy is that we have usually not understood that we are responsible for what we are heard to say-and its effects go far beyond our intentions and reach.

Far beyond the realms of the church and the Christian com-munity, there is a growing, rather ugly type of anti-Semitism in Japan, for example. Why should there be anti-Semitism in Japan? It has something to do with the oil, I guess, but why would it take the form of anti-semitism of a Western type? Since the Christian community has shaped Western culture, anti-Semitism (with the image of Jesus lambasting those dumb Pharisees) has become part of the cultural Western matrix. It isn't easy to retrieve such imagery. And the other cause for anti-Semitism in Japan is Shakespeare, the great cultural hero of Anglosaxon culture. He became one of the bearers of anti-Semitism wherever Western culture in its higher forms reached the world.

II

As we consider Christian preaching, we should start with the fact that Jesus is, of course, a teacher in the Jewish tradition--prophetic, eschatological-apocalyptic. I think I heard too little in the presentations this morning about the eschatological-apocalyptic dimension of the teachings of Jesus and that strand of early Christianity. It so happens that that is one which was palatable neither to the Jewish tradition as it consolidated itself nor, actually, to the mainstream of the Christian tradition as they consolidated themselves.

But Jesus was in the eschatological-apocalyptic tradition which was strong in many groups, and sects, and non-sects in the Judaism of his time. In that mood and mode Jesus spoke, even lambasted--that was part of that tradition. Here I would take issue with Michael Cook. I would claim that there is not a single statement ever reported in the name of Jesus in the synoptic gospels that is sharper in its critique of Judaism than what is proper for a prophet, and especially for a prophet of a high eschatological and apocalyptic intensity. We can point, for instance, to the Qumranites--the Dead Sea Scroll community--who expressed the most lambasting attitudes toward those "slippery interpreters" (as they called the Pharisees). We might like the style or we might not, but that's irrelevant. Precedents are plenty.

I have come to recognize more and more how significant and indispensible is this element of criticizing the foibles of religious folk. One eye-opener for me was a study of the "Sermon on the Mount" as it occurs in edited form in Third Nephi (one of the books in the Book of Mormon). There we find retold rather adequately the teachings of Jesus in the Sermon on the Mount, but without Jesus' critique of the Pharisees. Here is a Jesus who never says anything about the foibles of religious folk, of people who try to be serious in their faith. Instead, the style has been transposed into a text in which the only thing that matters is that one believes in Jesus, a theme familiar from the Gospel of John, but absent from the Sermon on the Mount, and from the thrust of the teaching of Jesus according to the synoptic gospels.

At first it strikes you as good news indeed to find a Jesus tradition without the critique of the Pharisees. In his comments on the Book of Mormon, W.D. Davies has rightly hailed this phenomenon.[2] But thereby Jesus is actually lifted out of the Jewish matrix within which he lived and taught. Instead of being a teacher in Judaism in the tradition of the prophets with eschatological intensity, Jesus becomes the "Revealed Revealer," uttering revelatory discourses concerning himself-- a certainly non-Jewish phenomenon.

Thus we must recognize--not least for the purpose of Christian preaching-that the anti-Semitism of the New Testament is not to be found in the critique of Jewish piety, as we find it in the teachings of Jesus. Take, for example, these words: "Jerusalem, Jerusalem, how often have I wanted to gather your children as a hen gathers her chicks under her wings; but you would not! Lo and behold: your house is foresaken!' (Mt. 22:37-38/Lk. 13: 34-35). That sounds pretty prophetic-apocalyptic to me. The decisive point is this: when Jesus spoke those words (as I think he did), he identified with the people. He spoke as a Jew to his own people. I think he lived up to the standard of a true prophet, which-according to Father Panikkar-is that a true prophet of doom prays like mad that he or she be proven wrong. Otherwise, that prophet is on an ego-trip-and there have been a lot of such "egotrip" prophets.

That was Jonah's problem, as you remember. Jonah-strengthened in his feeling of being a prophet by the unusual transportation God supplied-prophesied doom over Nineveh. But then God changed his mind, "repented of the evil which he had said he would do to them; and he did not do it" (Jonah 3:10). So Jonah had a professional crisis-his prophetic ego was hurt for he had been proven wrong. And God says to Jonah: "Should you not be happy that Ninevah is saved--120,000 persons and also much cattle?" The book of Jonah ends with those words "and also much cattle." I doubt that Jonah had even thought of the cattle--he was into the I-Thou business. But the main point of the story is that Jonah had not been a true prophet i.e., hoping that his prophecy of doom be proven wrong, iden-tifying with the people.

I think that nothing would have gladdened Jesus more than if the tables had turned, and the destruction would not have come. But what happened in the Christian church and in the editing of the gospels is that words against the Pharisees and the Scribes and against the establishment in Jerusalem "fell into alien hands." Now they were hurled with glee by the Christian community against the Jewish community across the street. Thereby these prophetic utterances were ruined, became venemous, and fed into the conceit of those who now knew themselves to be on the "right side." Here is one of the roots of New Testament anti-Semitism: Words spoken by Jesus as a Jew identifying with Israel-now being used with glee as signs of superiority.

The Christian preacher must be aware of how this mechanism is at work in the Christian tradition, and already within the covers of the Scriptures. When such an awareness becomes a part of our reading of the New Testament, we come to recognize that what I have called the foibles of the Pharisees are not "Jewish" but plain human foibles that tend to go with all of us as we try to be good, religious, serious, Christian, and first rather than last. If our awareness leads us to the study of Talmud and Midrash-or to mere listening to the teaching and stories of the Rabbi in town-then we shall recognize that the Pharisees themselves were no mean critics of exactly those foibles, and of the dangers of not seeing the forest for the trees. As Hillel put it: The Golden Rule is it--all the rest in commentary...

III

The great continuity with the Biblical tradition, as we heard already, lies in Jesus' proclamation of the Kingdom. Of all themes in the Jewish tradition--or, if you have a higher Christology: of the trillions of possible themes in the mind of God--Jesus chose the Kingdom as his theme. Thereby Jesus indicates what he is about: a redeemed and mended creation. When people come rushing up to Jesus and say, "What shall I do to inherit eternal life?", Jesus does not really answer in those terms. Eternal life is not a central issue for the synoptic Jesus. It is too self-centered, I guess. Jesus was after the Kingdom. That is what the Lord's prayer is about, as are its parallels in the Jewish prayerbook.

Here I would like to lift up from Paul van Buren's presen-tation, and lift up very high so that we see clearly how he described the aim of the exercise--what it is all about; the redeeming of the Creation, the completion of the Creation, the mending of Creation. This creation, when created, was pretty good, but it went downhill already in chapter three of Genesis. Ever since, God has been working on mending his Creation. That is what it is about. I mean, the first thing God thinks about when God wakes up in the morning is not: How many Christians are there? God wonders what the powers toward the mending of the Creation might be. Seek ye first the King-dom and God's justice-and the rest will somehow fall into place-the salvation of souls and little things like that, i.e., "all the rest." The issue is the mending of the Creation. That is what the Kingdom stands for. It came so natural when Paul van Buren spoke, so I just wanted to make sure that you understood that although it came so natural-or: since it came so natural-this vision of the overarching theme from Genesis to Revelation is of decisive importance for Christian preaching and Christian theology.

IV

In dealing with such material we should watch our constant urge to control the "patents" and the "copyright" of Jesus. We have this desire, even obsession, to know what is new with

Jesus. Even when the parallels with contemporary Judaism are striking, we cannot rest until we have found a difference of drastic import.

Behind such a habit of thought and research I detect not only general apologetic needs but also a view of reality more congenial to the career struggles of the academic world than to the life and ministry of Jesus. I am referring to the presupposition that the center, the heart, the inner core of Jesus' teaching lies at the point where he differs from all others. That is why students of the historical Jesus set up the problem this way: What neither the church liked nor can be found in Judaism before Jesus, must have been the real nucleus of the historical Jesus. That Jesus could think that something was truly important even though he did not invent it, is a strange idea in the academic world where you get tenure positions by coming up with a new idea, and where therfore one's ego, one's identity, is in that where he or she differs from others. I think the whole preoccupation with what was new with Jesus is a preoccupation that is alien to the culture of the time of Jesus, and alien to Jesus himself. It functions in our lives and in the life of the churches so that we can feel superior on Jesus' behalf. My conviction is that he does not need such P.R., and that the most central teaching of Jesus was in continuity with God's ancient urge toward a mended creation.

It is this continuity in the basic teaching of Jesus that leads me to stress that in the teaching of Jesus we have things that either were taught by the rabbis, or could have been taught by the rabbis. I am also intrigued by the fact that there is nothing in the Lord's Prayer that a Jew cannot pray with a whole heart. That does not mean that you should rush up to a Jew, and say: "Let's now say the Lord's Prayer together. I just heard a lecture which said that the Lord's Prayer was a perfect prayer for you."

We must also remember how prayers take on symbolic reality, and the Lord's Prayer is after all the prayer of the Christian church. Even so, I have always been intrigued by the fact that, in the Christian tradition, this is the only prayer to which the church does not add "in the name of Jesus Christ," but rather came to pick up a doxology from the book of Chronicles, of all things: "For thine is the Kingdom and the Power and the Glory" (cf. 1 Chr. 29:11-13).

When we preach on the Lord's Prayer as given by Luke's gospel we might even point out that Luke introduces the Prayer by telling about a question from the disciples (Lk. 11:1ff.). John the Baptist has given his disciples a badge, a kind of guild prayer, which is their prayer--you know, a sort of secret handshake with God--"their prayer." So the disciples ask, "please give us one too." And Jesus answers by giving them a prayer which is dealing with basic themes of Jewish expectation of the Kingdom--nothing "Christian" whatsoever, not even "Jesus-ish." So, when they wanted to have a prayer to set them apart, he gives them a prayer that links them closer to the great Jewish theme and plan, the mended creation, the coming of the Kingdom.

V

The Pharisees figure so prominently in the gospels because they were, when all was said and done, the ones to whom Jesus was closest. That is the way it usually is in material of this kind. It is, of course, well known that many or all of the issues that Jesus dealt with had also been dealt with by the Jewish sages. There is no question about that--"And you have heard that which was said to the ancients, but I say unto you..." In case after case, we can find in the study of the Rabbinic material the same awareness.

The Golden Rule is, of course, classic. Hillel had it also. Exegetes often point out--and we hear it in sermon after sermon--that Hillel said: "Whatever you <u>do</u> <u>not</u> want the other fellow to do to you <u>do</u> <u>not</u> do it to him..." Jesus, on the other hand, had it posi<u>tive.</u> Once that has been said, it gives such a lift to the Christian preacher that she or he stops thinking. Let me make two comments--legitimate after-thoughts. The first one is the sobering observation that the Golden Rule seems to have been used primarily in its negative form in the early church (Didache, Codex D in Acts 15:20, Irenaeus, etc.). So at least the early church did not understand that the great divide between Christianity and Judaism was the positive versus the negative. Of course, it is a classic strategy of liberal theology to assign an I.Q. of 90 to the disciples: that gives you complete freedom to correct them and get your Jesus as you like him. But I think that the uncritical joy in the commentary footnotes, when a lever like that of the positive Jesus is found, is suspicious in itself.

The other observation I offer with less certainty, but it has been suggested that the context of Hillel's formulation is the greater weight of precision that pertains to the prohibi-tions as compared with the more open-ended urging of positive commandments. Thus Hillel would say that even all those higly specific prohibitions are summed up in the Golden Rule. In any case, before we celebrate the superiority of our tradi-tion, we better get our facts straight.

Actually, in dealing with Jewish-Christian relations, as well as with relations to any other religion, we should medi-tate carefully on the ninth Commandment: "Thou shalt not bear false witness against your neighbor." I would say that 90 percent of what is called apologetics is a breech of that commandment. It's our common way of making our own faith great by telling negative stories about others. It's a need that we have to come out on top. It's a sign of people insecure in their faith.

I preached in the Hendricks Chapel here at Syracuse University yesterday.* It was about John the Zebedee who came rushing up because he was jealous on Jesus' behalf (Mk. 9:38-41), just as Joshua had been jealous on Moses' behalf (Num. 11:26-30; about Eldad and Medad), because there were some people who did certain things in the spirit of God, in the spirit of Christ, without belonging to "our" company. They had this kind of feeling that they needed to protect Jesus, to protect Moses. We have an expression in Swedish: "It's pathetic to hear mosquitoes cough." When I hear little apologetic attempts like that, I think of that saying: somehow, it's pathetic. And much of our preaching, which cannot rest until the superiority of Jesus has been shown, is of that category-totally unnecessary. The important thing is what is the will of God. I hope I have somewhat made that point clear.

VI

In the gospels the "Pharisees and the Scribes" have become stylized. In Matthew, for example, these terms do not refer to the actual Pharisees or the Scribes anymore, but are catch-words for the Jewish community-the synagogue across the street. They have lost their rootage in the original historical situation. That is how language functions. We all have a tendency of doing such things. In Luke, the Pharisees and the Scribes seem to be the example of the wrong piety which is opposed to the simple piety of the people-in the beginning of the Gospel of Luke, the pious people, Simeon, Hannah, etc.

The Johannine gospel is often referred to as the one with the most animosity toward the Jewish community. I beg to differ. I think something much more terrible has happened in John. I do not think John cares a bit about the Jews anymore, one way or another. He uses "the Jews" as a cipher. He takes a people and so denigrates it that it becomes just a symbol for the world, Evil, the realm of Satan. Actually, that is the ultimate insult to a living people. I believe that the RSV historicizes the text with its translation, "He came to his own home, and his own people received him not," but the Greek says, "He came to his own (ta idia) and his own (hoi idio) received him not." I think that is gnostic in its over-tones and refers to the cosmos and its inhabitants. For

*Unfortunately this sermon was unrecoverable for inclusion in this volume.--The Editor.

in John there is gnostic language which has swallowed the historical reality so that the Jews are just a chip in another's game. And that is, in a way, how the Jews have functioned-as we have heard today-in a lot of theological thinking through the ages. But in the Johannine gospel we see that principle at work most strikingly.

VII

A few years ago, I had the opportunity to deal in detail with responsibility of Chrisitian preaching in Holy Week, i.e., concerning Passion Narrativaes of the gospels. No Christian preacher should embark on that task unaware of the memory in the Jewish community that it was out of sermons in Holy Week that the pogroms began.

Much can be said about the various manners by which the gospel story about the passion developed, increasing the guilt of the Jews and minimizing or whitewashing (cf. Mt. 27:24) the responsibility of Pontius Pilate. Thus it has become increasingly difficult for the Bible-reader and for the preacher to recognize that the original story was one where Jesus came up against the Establishment (the high priests and the elders-not the Scribes and the Pharisees with whom he had debated in Galilee). And this Establishment behaves like establishments do. I can see those council members telling their wives about the long night-session: "We had a very difficult case. We tried our best, but he was so stubborn, so finally we had to deliver him to Pilate-for if he were to stir up trouble, the Romans would find a pretext to take away the little independence that is left to us."

That old saying of Caiaphas--"You do not understand that it is expedient for you that one person die for his people lest the whole nation perish" (Jn. 11:50)-is actually a timeless formula for the way the establishment does-has to?-reach its decisions. Which is to say that there is nothing particularly "Jewish" in the decisions of the Jerusalem authorities. Both they and Pilate are actors in a perennial and ubiquitous human drama. Only in an antisemitic community is it possible to find pictures and plays in which Judas or Caiaphas look more Jewish than Jesus.

VIII

And now few comments on the Apostle Paul. For reasons easy to understand, Paul is a thorn in the side of the Jewish community. Partly following some signals of Christian scholarship without detecting their antiJewish biases, Jewish scholarship by and large casts Paul in the role of the villain: the apostate who polluted Hebrew monotheism by making Jesus a god, and who turned against the Law out of his various frustrations.

On more careful inspection, however, Paul turns out to be the New Testament writer who has thought through the relation between Israel and the church in a manner that promises a renewed attempt at Jewish-Christian relations without contempt but in a mutual respect under God. (As Paul said in another setting, the thorn may turn out a blessing, 2 Cor. 12:7 and 9.) For Paul, the apostle to the Gentiles, is the first to perceive that perhaps the will of God in its full and positive sense was that the Jesus movement would become a Gentile movement. In his programmatic reflections on his mission and God's promise to Israel, Paul reaches this conclusion (Rom. 11:11-36). It is quite perceptive, not least in the light of the history we know. Paul sees it a mere 20 years after the beginning.

It is not unique that a movement born out of one setting comes to take hold and blossom in a drastically different one. Think of Marxism constructed for highly industrial European society by Karl Marx, sitting in the British museum. But Marxism first took real hold in the least industrialized, most feudal of all European countries, Czarist Russia--or was transposed into the agricultural situations of Mao's China. I am not saying that this explains all the mysteries of the world, but it is worth remembering that what actually happened to Christianity has its strong parallels throughout history-also outside the history of religions.

The Pauline insight that the Jesus movement was to be a Gentile movement is of great significance for our preaching. It is in Romans that Paul comes to this conclusion as he meditates on how his mission-to the Gentiles-fits into God's total mission, the "missio Dei". To this topic we shall return. Suffice it to note now that Paul's reflections seem to be triggered by his observation that Gentile Christians displayed conceit and superiority feelings toward Israel. But there is no reason for such. The salvation of the Jews is in God's hand in due time. In the meantime you Gentile Christians should stand in awe, without pride (11:20), recognizing God's mysterious plan which cancels out all "Christian" conceit (11:25). Such were Paul's mature insights about Jewish Christian relations. They came out of his experiences in mission. Thus they do not dominate all his writings-nor those of other segments of the early church as represented in the New Testament. But it could be argued-I would say: it should be argued-that this Pauline perspective is not just one perspective of many but the one to be given a primary role in our search for healing in Jewish-Christian relations. And that for two specific reasons:

a)   Paul was the first to spot the venom of anti-Judaic conceit in Christianity-and we of the 20th century know how right he was.

b)   The root of Christian anti-Judaism may well be somewhere close to the point where we define Israel as a non-entity, as obsolete and super-ceded--i.e., the very view that Paul criticizes in Rom. 9-11.

IX

In one way Judaism is, of course, most fully represented in Christian preaching by the Old Testament. Large parts of Christendom-including Lutherans to whom I belong-have a tradition which, until quite recently, almost never preached on the Old Testament. Strangely enough, we had to learn Hebrew. But apart from special occasions, on Sunday we preached on the Gospel in the morning and, if there was an evening service, we preached on the Epistle. Such was the structure of the Western mass. To be sure there had been other services in which there was ample use of Old Testament. But they came to fall out of parish use, and with them the Old Testament as a text for liturgical reading and preaching. In this respect the Calvinist tradition-including the role of Morning Prayer and Evensong in the Episcopal tradition--had a strong heritage of Old Testament usage in public worship, strengthened by the paramount position of the Psalms in Calvin's view of worship, cf. the Geneva Psalter.

I here use the term "Old Testament" consciously, since I like to focus on how the Torah, Prophets and Writings of the Jewish community, the "Hebrew Bible," functions in the Christian community. Lest Christians prescribe for the Jews how they should read "their" Scriptures, I think it is impor-tant to recognize that we do and we do not have the same Bible, and that the difference is not just the New Testament (or the status of the "O.T. Apocrypha"). We do relate dif-ferently to those same words from Genesis to Malachi, and the term "Old Testament" stands for that difference. (In a wider ecumenical setting, it should also be remembered that for a large segment of Christendom the Old Testament is not the "Hebrew" Bible but that the ultimate inspired authority rests with the Septuagint, i.e., the Greek translation. This is true for the Greek-Orthodox and other Orthodox traditions.)

I am belaboring this point since I think it is important for Christian preaching on the Old Testament to recover as Christians, ways to interpret the Old Testament in its own right, not only as negative background or mere prophecy of things to come. In pre-modern times "Old" had more venerable

connotations than it may have to our consciousness. I think
of the famous Matthean motto as a key to Christian preaching:
"Every scribe trained for the kingdom of heaven is like a
householder who brings out of his treasure what is new and
what is old" (Mt. 13:52).

     Sisters and brothers in the Christian faith: Abraham,
Creation, Exodus, and a lot of other things are quite suf-
ficient for a 20-minute exposition. And, in a certain sense,
"typology" is actually a kind of prescientific phenomenology
of religion. That is to say, there is the shape of God's
eschatological act, but it need not mean that the earlier
acts are thereby debased. There is nothing taken from Exodus
qua Exodus as the message of liberation by the fact that it
was in the night that he was betrayed that he celebrated a
meal which to us incarnates a liberation of cosmic dimension.
For the full wealth of the Scriptures it is very important to
learn to be revived in one's theology by the Old Testament in
its own right. The habit of reading the Old Testament as
"background," and especially background to Christianity,
leads to a strange blindness among preachers. On the more
liberal side of the Christian spectrum, where christology
plays less of a role, such blindness often leads to sweeping
affirmations that the God of Judaism in the Old Testament is
a God of wrath, while in Christianity and in the New
Testament God is a God of love. Such blindness can only come
from heavy preconceptions and self-serving biases. It is as
if the word "hesed" loving-kindness were not   in the Old
Testament-not to speak of the gruesome language of brimstone
and hellfire in the teachings of Jesus.

                              X

     Allow me a footnote concerning the Name of God, a note
made necessary by the recent revival of the name "Yahweh" in
some   translations.   I   consider   it   unacceptable
archaeological, antiquarian pedantary to reintroduce "Yahweh"
in English bibles intended for use as Christian Scriptures.
I remember some Bible translators in Thailand who raised this
question: "What are you doing over there in Europe and in
America; what is this dumb thing; do we not have trouble
enough without a personal name for God?" And the only thing
I could answer was, "I can tell you one thing- you are in
very good company. Jesus never said Yahweh." I think that
is a safe statement. Presumably he said Adonai/Lord or Ha-
Shem/the Name, but never Yahweh. Often this change from
Yaweh to Adonai is interpreted by Christians as rooted in
primitive fear of God. I prefer to see it as a fruit of
theological reflection, a change in spiritual consciousness
and a transcending of a stage of piety. In saying

Adonai/Lord we identify with that development and we should not be tempted by antiquarian pageantry. We should also note that by re-introducing Yahweh we drive an unnecessary wedge between the Jewish and the Christian Bibles.

XI

I wanted to return to the theme of the continuity of the Jews as a people. That is why I prefer to speak about Jews and not about "the Hebrews." I think we need to use the word that best expresses the continuity of the Jewish tradition because, as we have heard before, the real problem here may be exactly the Christian tendency of usurping the biblical continuity. Christians also need a sense of Jewish continuity, and we need the Old Testament for a very specific reason: As the book of the "long haul." The New Testament is the document of a short breakdown, a charismatic period in the history of God's people. Much of its glow comes from that fact. But the Old Testament is the "long haul" book. The "long haul" existence in faithfulness is a very different question from that of a high-pitched, charismatic zing and hope that can only be sustained for a short time. But in the Old Testament we have--for Jews and Christians--the pattern of God's ways with the people over the long haul, with ups and downs. Herein lies the necessity of the Old Testament to be read in its own right among Christians. We have been in for the long haul, we too by now. One cannot be a healthy community 2,000 years later, just by playing a first century charismatic enthusiast.

XII

The best way to take neighbors seriously is to be willing to learn from them. That principle certainly applies to Christian preaching as it strives to overcome anti-Judaic tendencies. Of course there is much to learn. Here I like to lift up an area in which we might be least prepared to learn from Judaism, that of universalism versus particularism. Christians in general think that it is much better to be universalistic than to be particularistic. Often we picture the Jews with their beliefs that salvation was just for them and as totally preoccupied with their own little thing (although we have slowly learned that that also somehow included the whole cosmos). In their particularism they are far inferior to us Christians with our universalism. But have you ever thought of the fact that it is exactly universalist religions that go on crusades? Have you ever thought of the fact that universalism so easily turns into a fanatic arrogance? As a universalist on behalf of Christ and

Christianity, it is hard to avoid the thought that it must be God's hottest dream that everybody become like me. Exactly for that reason universalism has an imperialist streak--and coupled with power an often violent streak.

It strikes me that the Jewish vision has a corrective for us. The Jewish vision of being faithful to God was that somehow God needed that faithful witness within the cosmic totality. Somehow, the faithfulness of Israel to Torah was needed by God as a light unto the nations-but that did not mean that all the nations should become Jews. Here is a great humility: to think about God and God's plan as one where one's own role is limited. I submit to you, that in a pluralistic world, in a world where we have many communities, in a world of universalist claims, universalism has a very bad record for oppression and suppression, be it of a capitalist or communist brand (both with their spiritual roots in Western Christianity).

It was, after all, the universalism of hellenistic culture that brought on the Maccabean revolt. The hellenistic rulers, the Seleucids, were going to bring those stiff-necked Jews into "modernity." Under the Romans, the Jews had it actually better, because Rome was really only interested in having a buffer toward the East; and the Romans knew that people were happier if they had their temples and their own traditions and things. So Herod was allowed to rebuild the temple in Jerusalem to keep the people happy. Marx called it opiate for the People. That was the Roman perspective also. But the Greeks had this kind of arrogance that "everybody who is cultured thinks like me." The cultural imperialism which lies in universalism is one of the real problems of the world. Thus we should perhaps take a second look at Israel's way of looking at its mission-being a distinct minority witnessing faithfully, God needing that witness in his larger plan. Humbly and obediently they knew themselves as a presence and a witness. I believe the early church thought of itself that way also. It was not their idea that the aim of the exercise was the Christianization of the world, but they did have the vision that now God was to have a new witnessing people, not based on Israel alone, but including a gentile community, across race and other barriers, constituted by faith in Jesus Christ. And we can learn from Maimonedes, who could think of Christianity and Islam as "bearers of Torah to the people." It is quite unique in the history of religions that one religion thinks of another religion in positive terms in relation to itself. Here is one thing we can learn from our mother Israel. As we become aware of the implicit danger of universalism, we may learn a style of presence. of witness without expectation of global victory for ourselves.

XIII

Allow me two more observations. "Anti-Semitism" today often disguises itself as "anti-Zionism." It is very interesting to compare this pattern of thinking with that of the 1930's. Of course, individual Jews are wonderful, and Judaism is a noble tradition, but the Jewish people... I would submit that our way of preaching about the Jew's expectation of the Messiah has much to do with this kind of thinking. We have preached so long something which goes roughly like this: "The Jews expected a political Messiah, but Jesus was a spiritual Messiah, and that is why they turned him down." With Zionism on the horizon-born out of Jewish despair about diaspora safety--people say: "So, there they go again, just as in the old days; they are looking for a political kingdom-Zionism-as if religious matters could be a question of real estate, etc., etc." The model fits only too well.

But I am far from sure that we have our historical facts right. Did the Jews expect just a political Messiah? The expectations concerning the coming of the Kingdom in the time of Jesus were far more complex. If I understand the Pharisees in the time of Jesus, they were anxious not to have the kingdom ushered in by political or military means. No, on the day when the whole of Israel kept the Torah, God would usher in the Kingdom. That does not sound political. Or again, those Qumranites were totally up in the clouds in apocalyptic expectations; "the war" was going to be fought by angels and archangels and all the company of heaven, and had little to do with a political gamesmanship. The Sadducees did not really want any change in the status quo, but were willing to live in a temple piety under the Romans. It was really only the Zealots, a very small group, that had the military-political vision. But we have created a model of ideas which now feeds into contempt for Zionism. That model will die hard. Finally, let us remember how the Talmud speaks of the Messiah: He is sitting among the poor lepers at the entrance of Rome, rebandaging their sores (Sanhedrin 98a). That just does not sound like a marshal, military, political Messianic image. That image, that Jewish image, would remind us how our preaching often is based on a totally free-hand drawing. We based it on the entry of Jesus on a donkey, but we had no serious interest in asking how that Messianic tradition lived within Judaism.

XIV

And, finally, let us consider, "In no other name is there salvation but Jesus" (Acts 4:12). That's what it says.

Peter, brought before the authorities, is asked and he answers, "In no other name is there salvation but Jesus." But we often forget what the question was to which this answer was given: "Did you do this miracle in your own name?" , and Peter says, Heavens, no "in no other name is there salvation but Jesus." That does not quite seem to settle the question of the relation between different religious traditions, does it? But these sayings sort of get legs of their own, and start to walk around.

In our preaching we must come to understand that such statements are statements of love. They are cast in love-language. They are the way in which we express our enormous gratitude to Jesus, for the magnitude of what he has given us. But there is no necessity, is there, for us to spell out the negative side? It is and should be the nature of confessional language to sing our song to Jesus, fully and without any hesitation. But the task is to sing that song without feeling compelled to shout or insinuate curses over others.

Thus my final suggestion for preaching is that we, at all points, overcome the temptation to make our case, our Christ, our God greater by judging others. For Christ and God do not need such "help" from us. Also, here the word of Jesus is liberating: "Seek first the kingdom and God's justice"--and then the rest will somehow fall into place.

NOTES

[1]Krister Stendahl, "The Sermon On the Mount and Third Nephi," in Reflections on Mormonism: Judaeo-Christian Parallels, ed. by Truman G. Madsen. (Provo, Utah: Brigham Young University (1978), 139-154).

[2]"Israel, the Mormons, and the Land," in Reflections on Mormonism, 78-79.

[3]See my Holy Week, (Philadelphia: Fortress Press, 1974).

PART THREE:

The Jewish People in Christian Preaching –
A Homily

Chapter Five

THE CHURCH, THE SYNAGOGUE AND THE GOSPEL

Darrell J. Fasching

(This homily was based on the following readings.)

Isaiah 42: 14-21

I have looked away, and kept silence, I have said
nothing, holding myself in. But now, I cry out as a
woman in labor, gasping and panting. I will lay
waste mountains and hills, all their herbage I will
dry up. I will turn the rivers into marshes, and the
marshes I will dry up. I will lead the blind on
their journey; by paths unknown I will guide them. I
will turn darkness into light before them, and make
crooked ways straight. These things I do for them,
and I will not forsake them. They shall be turned
back in utter shame who trust in idols: who say to
molten images, 'you are gods'. You who are deaf,
listen, you who are blind, look and see! Who is
blind but my servant, or deaf like the messenger I
send? You see many things without taking note; your
ears are open, but without hearing. Though it
pleased the lord in his justice to make his law great
and glorious, this a people despoiled and plundered,
all of them trapped in holes, hidden away in prisons.
They are taken as booty, with no one to rescue them,
as spoil, with no to demand their return.

John 9: 1-41

As he passed by, he saw a man blind from his birth.
And his disciples asked him, "Rabbi, who sinned, this
man or his parents, that he was born blind?" Jesus
answered, "It was not that this man sinned, or his
parents, but that the works of God might be made
manifest in him. We must work the works of him who
sent me, while it is day; night comes, when no one
can work. As long as I am in the world, I am the
light of the world." As he said this, he spat on the
ground and made clay of the spittle and annointed the

man's eyes with the clay, saying to him, "Go, wash in the pool of Silo'am" (which means "Sent"). So he went and washed and came back seeing. The neighbors and those who had seen him before as a beggar, said, "Is not this the man who used to sit and beg?" Some said, "It is he"; others said, "No but he is like him." He said, "I am the man." They said to him, "Then how were your eyes opened?" He answered, "The man called Jesus made clay and annointed my eyes and said to me, 'Go to Silo'am and wash'; so I went and washed and received my sight," They said to him, "Where is he?" He said, "I do not know."

They brought to the Pharisees the man who had formerly been blind. Now it was a sabbath day when Jesus made the clay and opened his eyes. The Pharisees again asked him how he had received his sight. And he said to them, "He put clay on my eyes, and I washed, and I see." Some of the Pharisees said, "This man is not from God, for he does not keep the Sabbath," But others said, "How can a man who is a sinner do such signs?" There was a division among them. So they again said to the blind man, "What do you say about him, since he has opened your eyes? He said, "He is a prophet."

The Jews did not believe that he had been blind and had received his sight, until they called the parents of the man who had received his sight, and asked them, "Is this your son, who you say was born blind? how then does he now see?" His parents answered, "We know that this is our son, and that he was born blind, but how he now sees we do not know, nor do we know who opened his eyes. Ask him; he is of age, he will speak for himself." His parents said this because they feared the Jews, for the Jews had already agreed that if any one should confess him to be Christ, he was to be put out of the synagogue. Therefore his parents said, "He is of age, ask him."

So for the second time they called the man who had been blind, and said to him, "Give God the praise; we know that this man is a sinner." He answered, "Whether he is a sinner, I do not know; one thing I know, that though I was blind, now I see." They said to him, "What did he do to you? How did he open your eyes?" He answered them, "I have told you already and you would not listen. Why do you want to hear it again? Do you too want to become his disciples?" And they reviled him saying, "You are his disciple, but we are disciples of Moses. We know that God has spoken to Moses, but as for this man, we do not know where he comes from." The man answered, "Why, this is

a marvel! You do not know where he comes from, and
yet he opened my eyes. We know that God listens to
him. Never since the world began has it been heard
that any one opened the eyes of a man born blind. If
this man were not from God, he could do nothing."
They answered him, "You were born in utter sin, and
would you teach us?" And they cast him out.

Jesus heard that they had cast him out, and having
found him he said, "Do you believe in the Son of
man?" He answered, "And who is he, sir, that I may
believe in him?" Jesus said to him, "You have seen
him, and it is he who speaks to you." He said,
"Lord, I believe"; and he worshiped him. Jesus said,
"For judgement I came into this world, that those who
do not see may see, and that those who see may become
blind." Some of the Pharisees near him heard this,
and they said to him, "Are we also blind?" Jesus
said to them, "If you were blind, you would have no
guilt; but now that you say, 'We see,' your guilt
remains."

This theme from John has a long and tragic history of
being used by Christians as justification for the persecution
of the Jews. I refer to the blind man who is cured by Jesus
and is not only literally restored to sight but also recogni-
zes that Jesus is from God; is the Messiah. On the other
hand, this gospel story stresses that the Jews who can see are
really blind and refuse to acknowledge that Jesus is the
Messiah. It is this theme of the blindness of the Jews of
which I speak and which we must explore.

It is a theme that has found its way into the entire
history of Christian theology, Christian art and Christian
behavior. For example, there are two statues at the south
entrance to the Cathedral of Strasbourg (France) representing
the Church and the Synagogue. The Church is pictured as a
young woman wearing a crown, with her head held high in
triumph as if surveying her realm. In her right hand she
holds a staff with a cross at the top and in her left hand she
holds a chalice. The Synagogue, on the other hand, is
depicted as a weak, frail woman, her head bowed forward under
the weight of a spear which rests across the back of her neck
as a sign of her subjection. What is most striking about the
statue is that the woman is wearing a blindfold. She is
depicted as unable to see. Here we have this theme in art
-the blindness of the Jews. I have the guidebook, which
depicts these two statues in the Cathedral, here before me,
and the caption reads "the figures of the Church triumphant
and of the Synagogue with frail body, so touching in her deso-
lation and in her abandonment." This has been a constant and
tragic theme which has persisted throughout the centuries of

Christian history; the synagogue desolate and abandoned in her blind obstinacy.

Is it an accident, I wonder, that during this same period in which the Cathedral was constructed (between 1200 and 1440 A.D.), the entire Jewish population of the city, some 2000 Jews were led out to the cemetery on a Sabbath and burned (c. 1350 A.D.)? For two thousand years a dominant theme of Christian theology and preaching has been that Christians have replaced Jews as the chosen people of God. For 2000 years Christian theology and preaching has tragically exploited the theme that Jews deserve to suffer for their blindness and obstinacy.

Can we be proud that such great church fathers, theologians of the second, third and fourth centuries as Justin Martyr, Origen, John Chrysostom and St. Augustine, could hold that Jews are guilty of deicide, that to love God required hating Jews, that as John Chrysostom put it, Jews were animals fit for slaughter, that they deserved, according to Augustine, to wander the earth homeless and in suffering until the end of time, as a consequence of their blind refusal of faith in Christ?

Is it an accident that along with these teachings, Christians have systematically persecuted Jews throughout history? Or, is it an inherent consequence of such teachings? Is it an accident that in the fourth century St. Ambrose could defend the burning of a synagogue by Christians and threaten to excommunicate the emperor if he rebuilt it? Is it an accident that Jews in Spain, during the seventh century were ordered to either be baptized or else be exiled from the country, and that later in the same century (c. 694 A.D.) all Jewish rituals were banned and children of Jewish parents over the age of seven years were taken from their parents, baptized, and raised as Christians?

Is it an accident that during the Middle Ages in Europe it was customary to observe Palm Sunday by stoning a Jew's house and to observe Good Friday by slapping a Jew in the face? Is it an accident that during the first six months of the first crusade in 1096 A.D., one third of the Jewish population of Germany was slaughtered, or again in 1298 A.D., 140 Jewish communities were decimated and a total of 100,000 Jews were slaughtered? Is it an accident that in this same century the fourth Lateran Council of the Church ordered all Jews to wear special badges and live in restricted ghettos, a device that the Nazis later also used, but did not invent? Is it an accident that in the sixteenth century Luther could advocate burning all synagogues and throwing pig droppings on any Jew who invoked the name God in public? And is it an accident that Luther's statements could be republished and used by the Nazis in this century, without editing, as part of the Nazi campaign to exterminate six million Jews?

There are those who have said, and even today say, that at the "final Judgment" all Jews are going to Hell because of their blind obstinacy. But I say that God is not a Nazi and heaven is no quaint, comfortable little village of happy Christians - Christians eating and drinking and making merry next door to a concentration camp, while the grey ash of burnt Jewish bodies wafts gently over the village. The whole vision is so grotesque that it mocks the very gospel of God's love. It is blasphemy against God himself.

But what can we as Christians do? Can we ignore the words of Jesus in John's Gospel? Can we pretend they do not exist? No. But we can employ an ancient and time honored pre-scription of Christian faith: that, whenever you encounter something in scriptures which you do not understand or, at first glance, seems unworthy of God, then we should "search the scriptures" for other passages which may provide a deeper understanding of the true meaning.

Very well, let us do that, and let us begin at the beginning, with the situation at the opening of this morning's gospel. Jesus encounters a blind man and his disciples ask, "Who sinned, this man or his parents, for him to have been born blind?" Here Jesus offers us our first clue - that blindness has nothing to do with sin, but is rather, in a peculiar way, a special vocation. For Jesus answers that "he was born blind so that the works of God might be displayed in him." (John 9:2-3) It is true that at the end of this morn-ing's gospel Jesus speaks of the guilt of those who are blind but say they see. But it is a very peculiar sort of guilt, for in the twelfth chapter of John an explanation of the blindness of the Jew is offered which echoes the theme of this morning's first reading from Isaiah. John says that, "they (the Jews) were unable to believe because, as Isaiah says again, "He (God) has blinded their eyes, he has hardened their heart, for fear they should see with their eyes and understand with their heart, and turn to me for healing." (John 12:39-40) What is suggested here is that God himself is the cause of their blindness. It is God who has hardened their hearts and blinded their eyes.

But what can this possibly mean? What sort of perverse game is God playing? Paul also cites this same theme from Isaiah, of God blinding the Jews, in chapter 11 of his letter to the Romans (11:9-10). But he cites it to prove precisely Jesus' claim that blindness is not due to sin but is a special vocation given by God for the purpose of revealing his works.

Acknowledging this blindness which is caused by God, Paul asks: "Is it possible that God has rejected his people? Of course not, I, an Israelite, descended from Abraham through the tribe of Benjamin, could never agree that God had rejected his people, the people he chose specially long ago." (Romans

11:1-2)   He asks again, "Have the Jews fallen forever, or just stumbled?" and he answers, "Obviously they have not fallen forever, their fall though, has saved the pagans..." (Romans 11:11)

What does Paul mean their fall has saved the pagans? If you read Chapter 11 of his letters to the Romans carefully, you will discover that he means that it was God's intention that the Gospel be rejected by the Jews in order that Apostles, such as himself, be forced to take their message to the gentiles instead. If this had not happened, he argues, we gentiles would never have been included among the people of God.   Thus for Paul, the true purpose of the Gospel is to bring us as gentiles into the house of Israel. As a result of the Jews playing the role of those who do not see, we gentiles have been grafted, says Paul, like a wild olive branch onto the natural olive tree of Israel, to share with the Jews the status of God's people. (Romans 11:24) By being grafted onto Judaism we are in fact made holy. So Paul explains;

> a whole batch of bread is made holy if the first handful of dough is made holy; all the branches are holy if the root is holy. No doubt some of the branches have been cut off, and like shoots of wild olive, you have been grafted among the rest to share with them the rich sap provided by the olive tree itself, but still even if you think yourself superior to the other branches, remember that you do not support the root; it is the root that supports you.(Romans 11:19-24).

Paul then regards Christianity as the gentile branch of Judaism.   In his letter to the Ephesians he explains that as gentiles, "You had no Christ and were excluded from membership in Israel, aliens with no part in the covenants with their promise..." (Ephesians 2:12)   But the mystery that has been revealed to him, he tells us, is that "pagans now share the same inheritance, they are parts of the same body, and that the same promise has been made to them, in Christ Jesus, through the Gospel." (Ephesians 3:6)

What does all this suggest about the destiny of the Jews for Paul? He suggests that their blindness has meant riches for the gentiles since it brought about the reconciliation of the gentiles. (Romans 11:12, 15) He goes on to suggest that once all gentiles are reconciled, "the rest of Israel will be saved as well." (Romans 11:26)   And with this event will come the final resurrection of the dead. (Romans 11:15) Thus until the very end of time, the final resurrection, Paul expects the coexistence of these two communities, the natural olive branch of Judaism and the wild olive branch, grafted on of Christianity. So Paul goes on to explain that;

> There is a hidden reason for all this, brothers, of which I do not want you to be ignorant, in case you think you know more than you do. One section of Israel has become blind, but this will last only until the whole pagan world has entered, and then after this the rest of Israel will be saved as well. (Romans 11:25-26)

(Notice that Paul does not say then they will recognize Jesus as the Christ and be saved, but simply "the rest of Israel will be saved as well.") But even more to the point is Paul's further explanation that;

> The Jews are enemies of God only with regard to the Good News, and enemies only for your sake; but as the chosen people, they are still loved by God, loved for the sake of their ancestors. God never takes back his gifts or revokes his choice. (Romans 11:28-29)

What Paul is saying is that the Jews only appear to be enemies of God and the Gospel, that this is part of God's plan so that the Gospel would be taken to us as gentiles. Their blindness is "for our sake." But, in their own personal relation to God as Jews they are still his chosen people whom he loves. If we do not see that, then it is we who are blind.

In the light of this explanation from Paul, the words of Jesus from this morning's Gospel take on a new meaning.

> It is for judgment that I have come into this world, so that those without sight may see and those with sight turn blind. (John 9:39)

It is Jesus' vocation to turn those with sight blind in order that those without sight might come to see and enjoy the Good News. That is, Jesus came not to the Jews, who were already God's people, but as a Jew to us who are gentiles or pagans. Jesus came with the Good News that we have been grafted onto the house of Israel to share with the Jews the promises of God.

The blindness of the Jews is nothing less than the blindness of faith. It is the blindness of those who trust God to lead them, rather than their own sight. It is the faith of Abraham who sets out on a journey commanded by God, without knowing where he is going. (Hebrews 11:8) And that is exactly what we heard described in our first reading from Isaiah this morning, as God speaks to his people, the Jews;

> I will make the blind walk along the road and lead them along paths. I will turn darkness into light before them and rocky places into level tracks. (Isaiah 42:16)

God is indeed with our brothers and sisters the Jews, for "God never takes back his gifts or revokes his choice." (Romans 11:29)   And for this let us give thanks and praise to the Lord our God with deep gratitude, for as Jesus tells us, "Salvation is (indeed) from the Jews." (John 4:22)

PART FOUR:

Jewish-Christian Relations - Present Realities and
Future Prospects

CHAPTER SIX

JEWS, CHRISTIANS AND THE FUTURE: WHAT MAY WE HOPE FOR?

Samuel Sandmel

(From; We Jews and You Christians)

(Even if Christians are successful in re-visioning the Gospel so as to affirm the integrity of the Jewish people, what may we legitimately hope for? In this article Dr. Sandmel explores the fundamental differences of attitude and approach to life in these two traditions and puts forward what seems a modest hope - that Jews and Christians become good neighbors. But that is no trivial hope for two traditions who claim that the heart of faith is to love God above all and one's neighbor as oneself. It is a goal, without which, neither community can be faithful to itself. - The Editor.)

Creedal and Noncreedal Religions

Your [Christian] tradition contains creeds--short state-ments of what you essentially believe--and you recite these creeds in your worship services. While our [Jewish] tradition is marked by distinctive beliefs, these do not take on a creedal character; we have one well-known "creed," that of Maimonides, but it is one man's summation of the essentials of Judaism and not an obligatory prescription decided on by a convened body of authoritative persons. In your tradition belief was prescribed, and your theologians have dealt with the various divisions and subdivisions of that belief, thereby clarifying its meaning and import; our theologians have dealt preeminently with obligatory obedient conduct, in its various divisions and subdivisions, and have largely ignored the defi-nition and the clarification of the beliefs themselves. This statement holds true even though we Jews do possess some quan-tity of medieval Scholastic philosophy which is kindred to your Scholastic philosophy: the statement is true in the sense that the usual Jew is reared in practices and observan-ces, such as holiday or dietary rules, and ethical injunc-tions, but not in even elementary theology. You Christians, on the other hand, deal with God, the Christ, the nature of man, the import of sin, and the like. If a neutral observer were to ask one of you what he believes, he would answer in terms of creed or theology, while one of us, if asked, would answer in terms of our Jewish sacred days and our ethical precepts. In a word, in your tradition, faith is explicit, and conduct usually left undefined or only implicit; in our tradition faith is left implicit and the conduct made definite and explicit.

The rise of secular humanism constituted a challenge to some or all of your traditional beliefs, including your inherited view of the Bible; for us the same movement, toppling the ghetto walls, created the problem of how readily possible it was for Jews on entering an open society to maintain the ancestral customs which presuppose something of a closed society. In the great upheavals in the Reformation era among you, while there were attendant circumstances of political and economic affairs, the religious issue was the dominant one, resulting in a division among you as to whether salvation lies in the church, that is, in the institution, or instead, in the Bible. Religious reformation among us was much, much less profound, for it dealt with issues such as altering the length of the services, and whether to retain them entirely in Hebrew or translate some or all of them, and what traditional usages seemed still viable and still necessary. For us Orthodoxy is the full range of practice, Reform Judaism a reduced quantity, and Conservative Judaism less than Orthodox but more than Reform; the theological differences are secondary, and were historically a second stage, not the first. We have almost no figures in our history such as Augustine, John Hus, Luther, or Calvin; such theological phrases as "justification by faith" and "predestination," and "the total depravity of man" are entirely outside our direct orbit. To go a step further, our tradition has lacked the structure and authority which the Catholics among you have inherited in the Catholic Church. On the other hand, the Bible was never as directly central among us Jews as it is among those of you who are Protestants, for the Bible for us is mediated through the rabbinic interpretation of it.

In such senses, our approach to belief is significantly different from your approach. Very few of us Jews are academically prepared to discuss our Jewish beliefs in the same way that many of you Christians are; and when you and we begin to discuss beliefs with each other, we often manage more to mystify each other than to enlighten.

But beyond this matter which I have called approach, there is a resulting difference, that you possess a sense of fervor about your beliefs, since these are crucial for you, while matters of belief among us take on the character of academic questions. You feel the obligation of believing, while our reduced obligation in this respect is often interpreted, or misinterpreted, as merely that of knowing. Some of your Protestant denominations were split into two on the issue of

fundamentalism versus modernism relating to the divine origin
of the Bible; our splits have never been on such issues,
though such issues arose after the splits occurred. Can you
imagine one of you who is simultaneously a Roman Catholic and
a Unitarian? Among us, insofar as synagogue affiliation is
concerned, a good many American Jews maintain active membership simultaneously in Orthodox and Reform congregations.
If you comment that this latter seems fraught with incon-
sistency and even contradiction, then from your perspective
you are exactly right, but we Jews have seldom been deeply
oppressed by such considerations.

Significant Differences

One could go on to list other divergencies. For example,
in your tradition the church is the key institution and the
home subsidiary; for us the home is the key institution and
the synagogue subsidiary. You tend to weigh fellow Christians
on the basis of belief, with affiliation quite secondary; we
weigh fellow Jews on affiliation and participation, with
belief secondary. Sometimes we both fall into the error of
weighing each other by one's own suppositions, so that some of
us quickly conclude that your interest is in theological
hairsplitting on irrelevant topics (shades of your Erasmus!),
and some of you conclude that our interest is in the
peripheral concerns of religion, not the central ones. Some
of you, penetrating a bit into us, are dismayed that we seem
very mute on topics such as God's election, the covenant, and
the like.

Sometimes you find it a little hard to accept that among
us the doctrine of the Messiah does not occupy the central
place that it does among you. You wonder, too, that not only
do we not regard Jesus as the Messiah, but that we seem relatively indifferent to the messianic views in our tradition.
It is often very hard to persuade you that what you have meant
by the Messiah is quite different from what we have meant, for
your tradition greatly altered and amplified the conception
you took over from us. If some, or even most, of you are
bewildered that we Jews can abstain from "accepting" Jesus, an
equal proportion among us is similarly bewildered that you
"accept" him. The question of Jesus is a complicated one; I
devoted to it the short book mentioned earlier, We Jews and
Jesus. Let me say only this much here: when in the past you
persecuted us in his name, we could scarcely be expected to
honor and cherish that name. A schoolteacher once commented
to me that Jewish students seemed to him to "cringe" at the
mere mention of Jesus by name.

In parts of Europe, many of us completely abstained from
letting the name Jesus come to our lips. To you it has always

been the supreme name among names; to us it was often the name
through which terror arose among us.   You must not be
surprised that there hang on, among ordinary, random people in
our midst, unreflective vestiges from the past.   Yet, with
persecution diminished, a good many of us Jews have written
appreciatively about Jesus, though invariably about a man, a
Jew, and not about the divine Christ of your Christian tradition.   Your basic Christian suppositions provide a place for
Jesus which our basic Jewish presuppositions do not; Jesus
serves in your tradition in a role which does not at all exist
in ours.

But let me move on to try to sketch in a broad outline
these fundamental religious divergencies between us.   We have
in common the Old Testament.   It begins with the Five Books of
Moses.   For us, the central part of the Five Books of Moses is
the laws, described there as divinely revealed, which begin
with the Ten Commandments in Exodus 20.   What comes before,
especially in Genesis, namely, the creation, the flood,
Abraham, Isaac, and Jacob, and the enslavement and release in
Egypt, constitutes materials which edify us or inspire us by
motivating us to emulate personalities whose achievements we
celebrate, such as Abraham or Moses.   But the nub of our religion is to be obedient to the divinely revealed commandments
which begin in Exodus 20.   These provide us with our ceremonies and, beyond them, with our ethics.   In a way somewhat
comparable to your appending the New Testament to the Old, we
have appended to our Scripture what we call rabbinic literature, in which is achieved the extended application and
interpretation of the laws, ceremonial and ethical, to diverse
and multiplying situations, (The chief rabbinic literature is
the Talmud, a two-stage compilation, written after first being
oral, consisting of the Mishnah, recorded about A.D. 175, and
the Gemara, about A.D. 450-500; and the Midrash, a verse-by-
verse interpretation of the biblical intent.)   The point to
notice is that though the literature of edification, such as
the Psalms, abided among us, and our medieval scholastics produced religious philosophy, yet obedience to divine commandments has towered over these things among us.

You may remember that in A.D. 70, the Temple in Jerusalem
was destroyed, and it has never been rebuilt.   In the Five
Books of Moses, the building of that Temple was enjoined, and
it was to be presided over by hereditary priests (the Hebrew
word for priest, cohen, yields the frequent Jewish name Cohen,
and its variant spellings: Cohn, Kohn, Kahn).   Jews had
spread throughout the settled world long before 70; they had
taken the Bible with them, and, where necessary, translated
it, as into Greek in 250 B.C., and they had created an institution where they assembled to study Scripture, to which among
Greek-speaking people the Greek word "synagogue" became
attached.   Since the study of a sacred book tends to become
similar to prayer, the synagogue has been both a school and a

prayerhouse; the instructor in Bible was the rabbi which means
"my teacher." When the Temple was destroyed by the Romans in
70, synagogue and rabbi were already on the scene to substi-
tute for Temple and priest; moreover, organized, systematic
schedules of prayer replaced the scheduled system of sacri-
ficing animals which had prevailed at the Temple (and which
have been entirely missing from us since the year 70). The
rabbi was not a priest, but essentially a teacher and
interpreter of the Bible, and a lawyer or judge in the developing and broadening legal-ethical system. The Jewish view
about obedience to law can be put in this way: Deliberate
disobedience amounts to challenging God, and is unforgivable,
and in time God, not man, will punish such effrontery.
Accidental, unwilled disobedience is forgivable, and divine
forgiveness can be sought by man through repentance and
through man's atonement; moreover, a man possesses the capacity to repent and to atone, and the free will to choose
whether or not to conform to the laws, and then to do so.

You will recall, of course, that Paul had taught that the
laws, which, to repeat, begin in Exodus 20, were not the truly
appropriate way to live the righteous life, for, on the one
hand, a man was incapable of choosing to serve them; instead,
he found the laws prompting him to disobedience, and, on the
other hand, the laws were second-grade revelation, not comparable to the substance found in Genesis about creation, Adam
and Eve, and the patriarchs, especially Abraham. Paul taught
that the laws were no longer in force, and that the righteous
life was to be attained through man's complete submission of
himself to God. Paul called this complete submission "faith,"
and he found in Abraham, who, of course, lived before Moses,
the supreme example of the man who through complete submission
to God achieved righteousness without needing the laws which
came at the later time of Moses. (About a century after
Paul's time, the explanation arose that Paul had "abrogated"
only the ceremonial laws, not the ethical ones.) The consequence of subordinating the laws to the contents of Genesis
was a shift from the centrality of laws, as such, to biblical
"history." It involved a shift away from the Jewish assumption, something everywhere else unchallenged in Jewish writings, that a man could choose to observe the laws and succeed
in doing so. Christianity challenged the assumption that a
man could choose to observe the laws or could carry out his
choice. Whereas for us Jews the laws, as in Exodus, were
central, for Christianity the "history" of mankind in Genesis
supplanted that centrality of the laws.

Thus Christianity came to a different view of man from
that which we Jews had, and have. Specifically, Christianity
held that Adam, the forefather of all humanity, who sinned in
Eden, transmitted to all his descendents the guilt for his
trespass. Hence, sin (and evil) is inherent in all men, and
as a result, a man is by nature unable, alone and unaided, to

rise above sin. Abraham rose above sin, through his total
submission to God, and God graciously reckoned Abraham's
"faith" as righteousness; it is God alone who can redeem man
from sin. The coming of the Christ was God's way of providing
mankind's redemption from Adam's sin, for when the Christ died
on the cross, the death was an "atonement" for man's sinful
nature, available to all men who had "faith," that is, who
submitted themselves completely to God. Thus, while Jews held
that a man could by his deeds achieve religious rightness,
Christians, especially those to whom Paul had been the guiding
voice, have held that it is only the grace of God which can
bring man to his rightness. To the Christian, the man who has
not experienced the supernatural grace of God remains
unredeemed; the career of Christ Jesus is held to have brought
salvation to previously unredeemed man. To the Jew, man was
never lost in sin, and hence not in need of salvation in this
sense. This is what I meant by the statement that in Judaism
there is no such role for Jesus which exists, as it were, for
the Christ in Christianity.

But to proceed with the contrast implied above, of the
centrality for Jews of laws originating in the Bible, and the
emphasis on salvation history to the Christians, each
tradition possessed the divergent approaches, already in the
first Christian century, and then went on to develop them
quite separately of course, and always in increasingly
divergent ways. Jews embroidered the laws, Christians
embroidered the history of salvation; Jews continued to
attribute to man the obligation to observe the laws which were
progressively expanded and refined, firm in the belief that
man could do so, or else could repent if he slipped. You
Christians raised questions about the nature of man, and about
which men-surely not all of them!-would receive divine grace,
and you supplied the answer that supernatural grace came to
those individuals who were "predestined" for it. With the
passing of time, you Christians probed these questions all the
more deeply, raising issues such as whether man in any sense
had any freedom of choice at all, or whether God's grace
providentially either came into a man or abstained from doing
so. You Christians did not agree with each other: Augustine
(354-430) insisted that man can be "saved" only by the grace
of God, and only those out of the mass of men whom God had
elected to receive His unmerited mercy were saved; Pelagius,
who lived in the same era, taught that man could on his own
take the initial steps toward salvation, quite apart from
grace, and moreover, if man was in no way responsible for
either his good or evil deeds, the lack of responsibility
implied that there was nothing to restrain man from indulgence
in sin. The views of Augustine and Pelagius were
antithetical, in that Pelagius assumed man had some choice,
and Augustine that man had none. Pelagius, however, was
condemned as a heretic, and his opinions as heresies. I cite
Augustine and Pelagius only in capsule illustration of the

Christian probing into questions about the nature of man, of grace, of faith, the relevance of which is that such probing and such questions neither received comparable attention in Judaism nor resulted in the decision that some one view was orthodox and another heretical.

Judaism never produced creeds, that is, short, authoritative statements of obligatory beliefs; nor did it develop the inner organization out of which to proclaim with relative universality which view was orthodox and which heretical; even though much of this question of heresy or orthodoxy belongs to the past, you are nevertheless still capable of some division on the question. I do not think I exaggerate when I say that such metaphysical disputes among you are so far outside our ken as to be incomprehensible to us; equally incomprehensible to you are our disputes on tiny details in our practices. Indeed, the real situation between you and us about the metaphysical Christ is not even so deep as the difference of belief, for it scarcely goes that far; we simply do not understand you at this point, and you simply do not understand us. And those who have tried to clarify this, through the device of over-simplifying, seem only to have made the obscure even more unclear.

Similarity in Ethics

I do not see any great difference between us in the matter of what we both regard as ethics. We differ in our formulations about ethics, and in the weight we give to it in our respective traditions. We Jews never divorce ethics from religion; your tradition, deeply committed to ethics as it is, nevertheless has often managed to set it below your advocacy of total submission to God, and some of you even tend to dissociate ethics, "works," from your Christianity. Our chief differences, however, are not in ethics, but in theology, and in our respective manners relative to theology.

Religious Usages

Yet alongside the theological differences I feel the necessity of adding an oft-omitted consideration that I regard as of possibly equal weight. Religions do not exist in vacuums, but are carried by people. A religion presumes a religious community. Religious communities develop ways of doing things, norms, and criteria, and usages, all of which can be remote from specific theological doctrines, and in some of these usages, which can be constitute the warp and woof of a religion, we differ also. The celibacy of the Catholic priest is as strange to us as our Passover seder ("order"), a sacred meal, preceded by prayer and ultimately giving way to children's rhymes and the attendant humor, is to many of you. Your tradition has prohibited divorce, but by and large has come to tolerate it (except for those of you who are Catholics); our tradition has permitted it, but has uniformly discountenanced it. I believe that there is a broader, wider adulation of education among us than has existed or used to exist among you, and I do not intend by this an evaluation but only a description. In our tradition the highest rung in the social scale went to the man of learning, not to the man of wealth. We Jews scarcely know any limits to our partiality for education. In our own time, it is reported that we Jews, constituting 3 per cent of the American population, constitute 10 per cent of American college students.

The ascetic tendency is more pronounced among you than among us. Monasticism is unknown to us and we felt no need to formulate, as did you Protestants, a doctrine of "vocation," that is, that men are "called" for a diversity of forms of religious achievement, though this view is quite essentially like our own unformulated assumption.

I believe that we Jews have been so shaped that we respond to philanthropy, in the sense of charity, in an unparalleled way. Philanthropy is a primary constituent of our religion, not an outgrowth of it. Our term for charity reflects a unique transformation in the meaning and enacting of a word. The biblical term, tzedaka, means righteousness. In our post-biblical literature, and in our use of the word even today, it is altered to become synonymous with charity. In the medieval ghetto we maintained orphanages, old folks' shelters, funds for the sick, loan funds, outright support for the indigent, funds to provide dowries which in those days were the prerequisite for a poor girl if she was to marry, collections to maintain schools, and the like; indeed, we were prepared to make an emergency assembly of funds to ransom Jews either imprisoned by state authorities or seized by pirates. In the modern world in which philanthropy has become scientific, and perhaps too much so, I have known Jews to object to some procedures which have come about, but I have not known of, or heard of, any Jew who challenges the assumption that to be philanthropic is an essential mandate of our religion. Indeed, there are some Jews in our time who, finding no sense of personal relationship to the worship service in the synagogue, express their Judaism one-sidedly in philanthropy. Nothing in my experience or my reading leads me to conclude that your estimable Christian philanthropy is quite as central to the religion, or as markedly accentuated, as is our Jewish philanthropy among us.

You can read explanations about Judaism and Christianity which contrast a supposedly this-world emphasis in Judaism and other-worldliness in Christianity. The key to a proper understanding here is to focus on the word "emphasis"; it is incorrect to contrast the Christian and Jewish attitudes totally. Themes of otherworldliness are found in the traditional Jewish writings, and Christian ethical responsibility has obviously dealt with this world. Furthermore, traditions as old as Judaism and Christianity have naturally harbored historical periods in which the themes of this worldliness and other-worldliness, found in both traditions, have been heightened or lowered.

There has been a great decline in the West in the quantity of Jewish knowledge a Jew possesses. Your Jewish neighbor is scarcely apt to be so informed in Judaism as to be fully apprised of the long history of Jewish thought. Rather, he responds to general trends and general instruction in Judaism, as these are mediated to him from his attendance at synagogue worship or a synagogue school, and not from exact knowledge. Accordingly, he may tell you, incorrectly, that Judaism never had a conception of hell, when the fact is that it did, and that you Christians took it over and greatly elaborated it; he knows, though, that by and large hell has disappeared from our usual Jewish thought. Your Jewish neighbor is quite unaware of the depiction of heaven in some of our Jewish writings; this representation is much less extensive and complicated than it appears in your tradition, and is, instead, a kind of vague, indistinct belief among us. Again our traditional prayer book is committed to a belief in resurrection, but we Jews have often inclined to interpret it as immortality, just as you Christians have; the Reform Jewish prayer book has substituted immortality for those passages which in the old prayer book read resurrection, and neither concept is specifically emphasized. While our tradition includes the belief that reward or punishment for good deeds or evil ones can await the individual after death, by and large these are not vivid matters to Jews, and, not entailing obligatory belief (for we have no creeds or dogmas as such), they are interpreted quite diversely by both informed or uninformed Jews, or are often more or less ignored.

Only in a small number of us will you find the theme of denying the physical pleasure of this world, but overwhelmingly we Jews subscribe to the view that this world is a place which we must enjoy. Vows of poverty and celibacy which characterize Catholic clergy are totally unknown to us. So, too, unknown to us are certain practices or views which prevail among some of you (or at least once prevailed). We have no religious objection to the use of liquor, but an objection only to drunkenness. We have not objected to the use of tobacco, nor have we ever espoused "plain dress," that is, a hat without a hatband, or a suit coat without lapels. Our tradition would prohibit us from being gourmands, but never gourmets (and that is why "kosher" delicatessans in very many places tend to become gourmet shops). "Kosher" means something in between "proper" and "clean," and strictly speaking should be applied only to food originating and prepared in such a way as to conform with ancient regulations; in this sense, meat can be kosher (that is, beef, lamb or goat, properly slaughtered, but not pork or shellfish), but dill pickles cannot be kosher. In our time kosher has come to be extended to certain foods which are merely the traditional cuisine of large segments of our people, but by no means to all of us. Gefilte fish (stuffed, spicy fish) or kasha (groats) are foods that some of our forebears brought to the United States with them, but these are quite unknown to others of us. The standard joke of comparing one's wife's cooking with one's mother's is probably no more than a reflection of a tendency among people to cherish the flavors of childhood food; hence, many of us incline to so-called Jewish food, but even this can so vary according to the region of origin of one's European ancestors that a wife's cooking can completely fail to resemble a mother-in-law's in any way! Traditionally we Jews have kept dairy and meat foods separate from each other, and similarly we have used different kitchen utensils and dining-room china for the two. Many Jews in our time have come to disregard the traditional regulations about food, either totally, or partly and inconsistently (for example, some Jews who would never dream of eating pork will assent to eating the equally forbidden shellfish); some Jews will run their household in complete fidelity to the traditional food laws, but ignore them partly or entirely, outside the home. It should perhaps be stated clearly that since there has been no authority of persons in Judaism able to repeal traditional laws, the food laws remain in force, as it were, and Jews who do not observe them have let them fall into disuse. If your Jewish neighbor strictly maintains the "kosher" practices, he can enjoy your home hospitality short of eating your food. If that is his bent, you Christians should never assume that he is rejecting you or your hospitality, and you should understand the implicit inequality in that he can feel free to serve his food to you in his home, but not eat your food in your home. There would be nothing amiss, if you have the impulse to entertain a Jewish visitor, to ask him, without embarrassment, whether or not you might serve him food, and he will not be embarrassed to give a genial and honest answer.

The divisions among us Jews (Orthodox, Conservative, and Reform), which highlight some of the differences just recorded, are not easily to be equated as identical to the divisions among you Christians. By and large your divisions are theological, and thereafter have resulted in differences in practice; for example, first Protestants denied the validity of intermediary priests, and asserted the "priesthood of all believers," and then proceeded to abolish the "confessional." With us the divisions arose in the realm of practice, and only thereafter became theological. Orthodox Judaism seeks to maintain the traditional ways indicated in

Scripture, and spelled out in rabbinic literature, without change or reduction. Reform Judaism preferred to abbreviate the worship service, and to couch it in the language of the land rather than to maintain the traditional, universally Hebrew one, and to seat men and women together, rather than to keep them separate at worship, and to reduce the quantity of the inherited laws, and not to abolish laws (or customs) as such. By and large, Conservative Judaism is a reaction away from the alleged extremism of the reforms of the Reformers, and was designed to attempt to preserve a larger quantity, but not the totality, of the inherited practices. Only at a later stage did theological issues enter in, and by and large these were are first relatively peripheral (that is, they dealt with the personal Messiah and the return to Palestine rather than with God or the Bible), and only later did they become more centrally theological. Your Jewish neighbor will be much more aware of the difference in practice (the seating of men and women together, the use or disuse of the skull cap, known as the yarmulke) than he will about theological issues. Moreover, these divisions among us, though often felt intensively by the pulpit, are treated with elasticity by the pew, especially in the United States, and these divisions scarcely ever impede a maximum cooperation and Jewish unity in matters of philanthropy or health and welfare. Synagogue affiliation bears some relationship to the size of the city and the community; in general, Jews in small cities almost unanimously maintain a formal affirmation, and bear the financial responsibility; the larger the city, the less encompassing is the synagogue affiliation. In the very large cities there are Jews who are active in various phases of the Jewish community, who may neither attend a synagogue nor even maintain a nominal "membership." (Among some of you Christians, "membership" connotes a sense of personal religious experience, and does not relate to enrollment in a list of the affiliates of a given church; with us Jews, membership is strictly a matter of enrollment.)

Among some of you Christians, in particular Roman Catholics, church attendance is obligatory; in our tradition, synagogue attendance was expected of males, even though such expectation fell short of obligation, and our women were welcomed but not usually expected to attend. In this context it must be mentioned again that with you the center of the religious life is the church, and the home supplementary; with us, the centrality is the home where much of our religion is practiced and taught through time-honored ceremonies such as lighting the Sabbath candles, and the synagogue is supplementary. (There are however all too many of us Jews who have confused the lack of obligation to attend the synagogue worship with a presumed sanction for nonattending.) Just as among your urban Protestants, attendance reaches high points at Christmas and Easter, so among us there are the high points at the Jewish New Year and Day of Atonement.

This parallel is symptomatic. Western open communities tend to effect a kind of unconscious uniformity even among the diverse elements. For example, the Protestant minister is not a priest, but a layman; so too the rabbi is a layman, not a priest. Yet the trends in our complex urban life tend increasingly to make ministers and rabbis act as if they were priests, and to make the congregations more nearly akin to audiences than to active participants. The tendency toward such uniformity goes on apace; however, it scarcely affects those matters which might be described as the tone and texture of the attitude of an individual to his tradition. What this means is that if you are a Christian, you must not assume that a Jew has the same sense of relationship to his Judaism as you have to your Christianity, and vice versa.

Jews and Christians approach their cohesiveness differently. A writer has pointed out that the collective feeling of Christians for each other is to be describes by the word "fellowship," that of Jews by the word "kinship." Certainly our being fewer in number and our having, despite our inner diversities, a common history of persecution and of anxiety about persecution increase our sense of kinship, especially when the times are threatening. We Jews are quite capable of becoming seriously and even bitterly divided among us, but this divisiveness recedes or disappears when an external urgency compels it.

The Responses to "Modernism"

Jews and Christians also seem to approach and respond differently to the complex series of issues raised by the rise of modern secular thought, which coincided with the fall of the ghetto walls. You Christians have had to handle the problem of how you can maintain your traditional supernatural beliefs in the light of the emergence of an age which has so largely repudiated supernaturalism; our instinctive response has been the different question: How can we maintain in an open society those practices of ours which fitted so naturally into a closed society? Perhaps I might put it in this way, that in the light of your emphasis on theological consequences, you were confronted by theological issues when Darwinism appeared, and you had the problem before that of reconciling Galileo's teachings with church assumptions. We, on the other hand, have had very little difficulty in such matters (for even the traditional among us have not been bound to the literal wording of Scripture as most of you Protestants have been). Rather, we have been confronted by problems such as the ability to observe Saturday as the Sabbath in a social situation where it is not the day of rest, or how our children can attend a university in a small town which lacks a Jewish community and still be faithful to our food laws. The open community is hospitable (despite diminishing but continuing barriers) to us as individuals, but disruptive of our corporate traditional practices.

Lacking the decisive theological rigidity which has characterized many of you, we have had very little difficulty in embracing modern scientific theories, or modern learning, or modern literature or art. We are conditioned to find a distinction between the sacred and the secular of only minor significance, for we have viewed all facets of life as potentially sacred, and the sacred as permeating the secular. Lately some of your thinkers have, as it were, either discovered or rediscovered "secularism" and have been struggling to find some form of reconciliation or congruency of Christianity with it; this sort of thing is ancient with us, and to most of us no problem at all in a theoretical way.

Yet it is true that, theology aside, some Jews feel seriously threatened by the modern scene, and attempt to maintain, either little changed or totally unchanged, the characteristics of the social configurations of the closed medieval ghetto. Perhaps this impulse might be clearer if I mention a segment of the Israeli population which is at odds with the rest of Israel in that it preserves the medieval dress, the medieval Jewish education, the medieval attitude to woman, all this in a national state which is as modern and Western as any modern state, and whose universties, the Hebrew University and Technion, are as scientifically advanced as any Western university. These traditionalists-some call them ultra-traditionalists, for even among the traditionalists a range of elasticity or else rigidity has come about-are not so much in protest against modern science as they are in protest against the possible dissolution of the corporate Jewish life. Hence, whereas many Israelis have discarded traditional habits, such as the maintenance of the traditional tonsure (which curled sideburns), and incline to some disregard of the strictness of Sabbath prohibitions of riding or smoking on that day, the ultra-traditionalists will make no concessions at all. It can be correctly contended that theological issues are inevitably at stake and bound up in these matters. My point, however, is that the theological facet remains implicit and in the background, while the issues of protective practice occupy the foreground. It is in such a light that you can perhaps understand why some Jewish thinkers have expressed a preference to the term which describes traditionalism as Orthopraxy rather than Orthodoxy. The latter would imply unchanged belief; the former, unchanged practice.

Except for the ultra-traditionalists in Israel or in isolated localities in the West, Jews, whether they are Reform, Conservative, or Orthodox, feel completely at home in the modern scientific culture. Perhaps I should modify the last sentence so as to note that in the past two decades we Western

Jews have adopted from your theologians a beginning theological interest, as a result of which we have been breeding a
growing number of theologically minded younger men who
confront us with theological issues more or less comparable to
your own, including a Jewish "death of God." This new approach
is a necessary afterthought, it seems to me, to the complete
adjustment we Jews have made in the world of modern culture.
Now that we find ourselves at home in it, we consider it
necessary to inquire and understand where we have suddenly
found ourselves. Nevertheless, if I were to put into a simple
contrast the distinctive character of Christians and Jews
respecting a particular common problem, the Christian tendency
would be to ask, "What shall we think about this?" while the
Jewish tendency would be to ask, "What shall we do about
this?"

     Accordingly, there are many significant fine points,
which, unperceived, have kept us from readily understanding
each other's religions. Our misunderstandings, paradoxically,
have been increased by some common possessions which we each
use differently. The divergent use of the Old Testament,
whether the emphasis should be on the laws or history in it, is
only a single example. Beyond this, you and we quote the Old
Testament, but often interpret the same verse in contradictory
ways, and then we become puzzled that disagreement increases
instead of giving way to agreement. We have used so variously
elements which we have in common that we have often been
totally blind to our possession of common elements.

     Even beyond the abstruse questions of theological dif-
ferences, then, religious traditions take on a corporate shape
and develop particular motifs, and these latter, as I have
indicated, seem to me quite as significant in the distinctions
between religions as the theological. A problem that remains
to us is that we have each generally assumed that one of us is
totally right and the other totally wrong. I will return to
this matter, for it requires exposition and also candor, since
it remains an ongoing problem.

                    Limits to Religious Understanding

     Somehow, I become less and less sure that full religious
understanding is a realizable goal, especially on any broad
basis between your men in the pews and ours. I do not mean
that animosities cannot be largely reduced, and often eliminated, and that cooperation in common social ventures cannot
increase. But the more I try to press on to envisage genuine
and profound religious understanding, involving facts, ideas,
and a fair and balanced comprehension of them, the more I
become persuaded that parochialism and particularism can never
completely disappear, for they strike me as so deeply imbedded

as to defy eradication. I must risk offending by saying that you Christians tend to regard your Christianity as a pure universalism, but I wonder if your judgment here is sound and fair. In our Jewish tradition we have had eras of universalism and of particularism; with us the universalism has never extended to the point of liquidating the particular, nor the particularism ever to completely obliterating the universalism. I suspect that you are not any more universalistic than we are, but have merely substituted a new entity, "the church," or "Christendom," or "Christianity" for our inherited entity, the Jewish people. However universalistically you may reinterpret the phrase, "there is no salvation except in the church," the phrase remains, and I imagine that you will concede that there are those among you who hold to the literal import of the phrase, however much you differ on which denomination is to be regarded as "the church". I am by no means sure how far to universalism all of us Jews will go, for though I know that some will go a long way, I know that others will go scarcely any distance.

There is, of course, the possibility that within the confines of inevitable particularism, some individual persons can nevertheless be universalistic. If so, they are this way not because of the tradition, Jewish or Christian, but despite it. Indeed, when such universalistic persons arise, their impulses are apt to be humanistic, that is to say, the product of heightened humane qualities rather that the result of a religious mandate. Men are mixtures in many ways, and it seems to me possible therefore that a man can be fully universalistic, even while adhering to a tradition which by its nature falls short of universalism.

Universal Religion

The Judaism which I personally wish to preserve appeals to me as a religion of universal relevance. I live in a particular state, Ohio, and vote in it; I express my American patriotism through the vehicle of my Ohio residency. Ohio is the particular, but the nation, indeed mankind, is the universal. Judaism is my particular, through which I express my universals.

I think I am aware of facets of our corporate Jewish existence that I would change if I could. Indeed, I love my tradition deeply enough to be critical of it at points. But I know also its great depth and its tremendous moments and achievements. It is from a Jewish source, the literature of the pre-exilic prophets, that there emerged the first visions of a united humanity living in a world of universal peace. I cannot turn my back on this. I am sure that other Jews feel the same commitment with equal earnestness.

We Jews intend to remain Jews. Your Jewish neighbor intends to remain a Jew. We Jews welcome converts who seek us out; we do not go out seeking for converts, though perhaps we should. Your Jewish neighbor will in all probability send his children to a Jewish religious school, whether an all-day parochial school (which most of us Jews seem opposed to), or an after-school (which most of our children find burdensome) or a Sunday school (which almost all of us consider insufficient as a vehicle).

What does your Jewish neighbor want of himself respecting you? What does he want of you? The answer to both questions is the same: a good neighbor.

Two hundred years ago he could not have been your neighbor, nor you his. Two hundred years ago he was inevitably regarded as your enemy, and you his.

All this is in the process of change, and the change is already far advanced. What was not possible then is possible now.

Possible, but less than certain. Possible, but fraught with misunderstandings aggravated by occasional excessive sensitivities. Possible, but overshadowed by the traumas of the past tragic decades and by unwholesome incidents. Possible, already in our time. And who knows what even greater blessing the future might bring if each of us tries to learn and understand?

A SELECTIVE BIBLIOGRAPHY

The following is a brief list of some suggested further readings. It is not meant to be exhaustive. Some of the texts cited provide further and more extensive bibliographies.

Cook, Michael. Mark's Treatment of the Jewish Leaders. Leiden: E.J. Brill, 1978.

Borowitz, Eugene. Contemporary Christologies: A Jewish Response. New York: Paulist Press, 1980.

van Buren, Paul. Discerning the Way. New York: Seabury Press, 1980.

Davies, Alan. AntiSemitism and the Foundations of Christianity. New York: Paulist Press, 1979.

Eckardt, A. Roy. Elder and Younger Brothers New York: Schocken, 1973.

Fisher, Eugene. Faith Without Prejudice. New York: Paulist Press, 1977.

Flannery, Edward. The Anguish of the Jews. New York: Macmillan, 1965.

Fleischner, Eva, editor. Auschwitz: Beginning of a New Era?. New York: KTAV Publishing House, 1977.

----------------. Judaism in German Christian Theology Since 1945. Metuchen, N.J.: Scarecrow Press, 1975.

Klein, Charlotte. Anti-Judaism in Christian Theology. Philadelphia: Fortress Press,1975.

Littell, Franklin. The Crucifixion of the Jews. New York: Harper and Row, 1975.

McGarry, Michael. _Christology After Auschwitz_. New York: Paulist Press, 1977.

Pawlikowski, John. _What Are They Saying About Christian-Jewish Relations?_. New York: Paulist Press, 1980.

----------------. _Christ in the Light of The Christian-Jewish Dialogue_. New York: Paulist Press, 1982.

Peck, Abraham, editor. _Jews and Christians After the Holocaust_. Philadelphia: Fortress Press, 1982.

Ruether, Rosemary. _Faith and Fratricide_. New York: Seabury Press, 1974.

Sanders, E.P. _Paul and Palestinian Judaism_. Philadelphia: Fortress Press, 1977.

------------. _Paul, the Law, and the Jewish People_. Philadelphia: Fortress Press, 1983.

Sandmel, Samuel. _Anti-Semitism in the New Testament_. Philadephia: Fortress Press, 1978.

Sloyan, Gerard. _Is Christ the End of the Law?_. Philadelphia: Westminster Press, 1978.

Stendahl, Krister. _Paul Among Jews and Gentiles_. Philadelphia: Fortress Press, 1976.

Talmage, F.E., editor. _Disputation and Dialogue_. New York: KTAV Publishing House, 1975.

Thoma, Clemens. _A Christian Theology of Judaism_. New York: Paulist Press, 1980.

Index

Anti-Jewish stereotypes: church and synagogues, 81; Holy Week as a source, 69; in the gospels, 40-45; 68-69; Japanese use of, 62; interpretations of Jesus, 91; origins in misuse of prophetic criticism, 63-64; overcome by searching the scriptures, 83; Paul as resource for overcoming, 70-71; messiah as political figure, 75; messiah and zionism, 75; overcoming in christian teaching and preaching, 38-40; 200 years of, 82; thou shalt not bear false witness, 68

Auschwitz: 19; 32-33; 46;82.

Blindness: Jewish reaction to the theme, 9; see also scriptures

Chosen: remmant, 6; denial of Jewish choseness by Christians, 7

Covenant: broken, 7; gentiles included through Jesus, 30; Jewish, 3; with Israel, 5

Cross: links Christians to the God of Israel, 30

Circumcision: interpreted as punishment, 7

Creation in need of completion: 26-27; 30; 31; 65; 67

Dialogue with Trypho: 7

Denominational Divisions of Judaism & Christianty compared: 98-100

Epistle of Barnabas, 7

Eschotology: Jewish & Christian, 30; see also scripture

Fall of Jerusalem: 6; 7   31; 92-93

Final solution: xvi

Genesis: 65

Genocide: xvi

Gentile: definition, 23-24; gentile institution the church, 25; in Paul, 6; gentile way is not the Jewish way 25; influx into Judaism, xvi-xvii.

Golden rule: 65; 67

Inter-faith relations: 13-16; 87-104

Israel: the state of, 20-21; 101

Javneh: 23

Jews: in John and Matthew's Gospels, 42-45; plague of the human race theme, 8; problem of understanding and defining, 21; stereotyped, xv

Jewish problem: as a theme in Christianity, xvi

John's Gospel: references to: 22; 63

Law vs Gospel of Love: 15

Liturgy: see preaching, also scripture

Marcion: 49;50

Matthew's Gospel: 62-63

Messiah: age of, 26; as crucified is a contradiction, 29; and Zionism, 75; Christ as a proper name, 28; Christ is God as valid Christian statement, 52; Christ and Jesus in Judaism and Christianity, 92; Christian definition of christ fills no need in Judaism, 94; Christology is not Messiology, 29; days of, 28; Jewish vs Christian definition 4, 12-13; Jesus as Messiah, not to be found in Old Testament, 47; Jesus and the Messianic age as criterion for Messiah, 29; Messianic age not yet 49, 52-53; Messiah is not same as Christ: 28-29; Paul's Christology, 30; spiritualizing of Messiah in Christianity, 53; stereotype of political definition, 75.

Mosquitos: 68

Morman: Book of, 63

Names: Ambrose, 82; Augustine 82, 90, 94; Baum, Gregory, 46; Calvin, 90; Chesterton, 61; Cook, Micheal, 61, 63;

Chrysostom, xv, 8, 45, 82; Darwin, 100; Davies, W.D. 63; Eckhardt, Roy, 37; Erasmus, 91; Fackenheim, Emil, 32; Hallen, Douglas, 49; Hellwig, Monica, 46; Herod, 74; Hillel, 40, 65, 67; Hus, John, 90; Jeremiah, 49; John the Baptist, 60; Justin Martyr, 7, 82; Luther, 61, 82, 90; Maimonedes, 74; 89; Marx, Karl, 74; McGarry, Michael, 45; McKenzie, John L., 47, 48, 50-51; Moses, 8, 28, 32, 92; Origen, 82; Parkes, James, 45, 47; Pannikar, 64; Pawlikowski, John, 46; Pelagius, 94; Pilate, 29-30, 69; Ruether, Rosemary, 47, 52-53; Shakespeare, 62; Shammai, 40; Tillich, Paul, 49-50; Tracy, David, 49; van Buren, Paul, 53, 65; Wellhausen, J., 50; Zakkai, Johanan ben, 23.

Negative witness theory: 19-20

New Israel: 4-6

Other worldiness: Jewish & Christian views, 96-97

Particularism and Universalism: 73-74; 102-104

Paul: as resource for healing Jewish-Christian relations, 69-71; Jesus subordinate to God, 30; Jewish reaction to, 9; remnant theory of 16; the law and sin, 93-96; theology of, 5-7; use of Hebrew scriptures 48.

Pharisees: and Ezra's reform, 23, 25; and Jesus' teachings, 67; Essene view of, 63; establishment behavior of 69; human foibles, not Jewish foibles, 64; overcoming sterotypes of, 38; response to Christian exegesis of its scriptures, 8, 11; stereotypes of, 39-40, 62, 68; Wellhausen's thesis, 50; were self-critical, 65

Preaching: Holy week as a problem, 69; promise and fulfillment as a liturgical theme, 46-54; stereotypes in liturgy and preaching, 37-45; use of O.T., 70-72; we are responsible for what we are heard to say, 62; word of God as preached rather than as bible, 61; see also scripture

Romans 9-11: xvii, 5-6, 30, 52, 70-71, 83-84

Rejection of the Jews: 5-7

Righteousness: Paul and the rabbinic interpretation, 9-10

Revelation: as developing, 31-33; from Auschwitz, 32-33

Reformation: 90

Sabbath: 7; 40

Scripture: a strategy for ovecoming stereotypes from, 83; anti-Judaic "heilsgeschicte interpretation, 50-51; anti-semitism in the New Testament, 11-13, 45ff; Bible has ugly things on its conscience, 61; book of Jonah on prophecy, 64; blindness of Jews, 79-86; Christian reinterpretation of Jewish scriptures, 22; Christian scriptures as cause of anti-Judaism, 13-15; confusion due to different interpretation traditions, 102; God of love and wrath in both testaments, 72; Jesus' prophetic language in N.T., 63; Jesus teachings as rabbinic, 66; Jewish and Christian-gentile approaches to, 24-25, 94; Lord's prayer as Jewish, 66; Kingdom of God unites Jesus to Judaism 65; names for God that are preferable to Yahweh, 72-73; new covenant theme, 5; O.T. and N.T. redefined as Hebrew scriptures and apostolic writings, 31; O.T. as the long haul book, 73; O.T. as useful term, 71; O.T. as used in

christian preaching and
liturgy, 70-72; problem of
lay interpretation, 13-15;
promise and fulfillment
theme, 46-54; rabbinic
interpretation and Christian
interpretation, 9, 14;
reforming use of O.T., 47-51;
revelation and the Bible in
Judaism and Christianity, 31-
33; revelation as ongoing,
31-33; salvation in Jesus
name only, 75-76; sermon on
the mount, 62-63; stereotypes
and liturgical use of, 37-45;
Talmud as parallel to NT, 92;
Torah, from Abraham to Jesus;
24; typology and allegory,
48-49; Wellhausen, 50ff; word
of God in preaching rather
than Bible, 61.
Secularism: xvi; 15; 21; 100ff
Shema: 26
Sin: Jewish and Christian views,
93-94
Spirit: God as, 26
Spiritual genocide: xvi
Strasbourg Cathedral: 81
Suffering Servant: 9
Supercession: XVI,
4,5,19,20,22,50,66,70,73,82
Theology: Jewish and christian,
101-102
Trinity: a gentile definition
of the God of Judaism; 26-28;
God as three persons misun-
derstood, 27; Jesus is God as
a Christian claim, 28.
Twin movements: Judaism and
Christianity in 1st century,
23.
Universalism & Particularism:
73-74; 102-104
Vatican II: 20, 37-39, 52, 53

Scripture Index

Acts	4:12	P. 75
Acts	15:20	67
I Chronicles	29:11-13	66
1 Corinthians	15	36
2 Corinthians	12: 7-9	70
Deuteronomy	6	49
Ephesians	2:12	84
Ephesians	3:6	84
Exodus	20	92
Exodus	20	93
Hebrews	11:8	85
Isaiah	42:14-21	79
Isaiah	42:16	85
Jeremiah	31:31	5
John, Gospel	4:22	86
	9:1-41	79
	9:2-3	83
	9:39	85
	11:50	69
	12:39-40	83
Luke, Gospel	11:1ff	64
Mark, Gospel	9:38-41	68
Matthew, Gospel	5:23-24	62
	13:52	72
	22:37-38	66
	27:24	69
Numbers	11:26-30	68
Romans	11:1-2	84-85
	11:9-10	83
	11:11	84
	11:12 & 1	84
	11:19-24	84
	11:24	84
	11:25-26	85
	11:26	84
	11:28-29	85
	11:29	86
Zechariah	8:23	27

CONTRIBUTORS

Dr. Michael Cook

Associate Professor, Hebrew Union College

Michael Cook received his undergraduate training at Haverford College where he graduated magna cum laude in 1964. Following study at the Hebrew University in Jerusalem, he earned an M.A.H.L. and ordination from the New York campus of the Hebrew Union College, Jewish Institute of Religion in 1970. His doctoral work, pursued at the Cincinnati campus of HUC-JIR, focused on the history and literature of the period of the Second Temple, with a specialization in the area of New Testament. Dr. Cook's publications include the articles on "Judaism, Early Rabbinic" and "Judaism, Hellenistic" in the Interpreter's Dictionary of the Bible (Supplementary Volume), also "Jesus and the Pharisees: the Problem As It Stands Today," Journal of Ecumenical Studies 15 (1978); and a book, Mark's Treatment of the Jewish Leaders, (Leiden: E. J. Brill, 1978).

Dr. Paul van Buren

Professor of Religion, Temple University

Author of a number of books and articles, Paul van Buren is probably best known for his book The Secular Meaning of the Gospel, NY: Macmillan Co. 1963. His most recent works have been two books dealing with Judaism and Christian theology: The Burden of Freedom: Americans and the God fo Israel, NY: Seabury Press, 1976, and Discerning the Way: A Theology of the Jewish-Christian Reality, NY: Seabury Press, 1980. Dr. Van Buren served as chairman of Temple University's Department of Religion from 1974 to 1976. He was Tantur Lecturer at the Ecumenical Institute in Jerusalem in 1977. He holds a B.A. from Harvard Univesity, cum laude, 1948; BD from the Episcopal Theological School, cum laude 1951 and a doctorate in theology, Universitaet Basel, summa cum laude, 1957.

Dr. Darrell J. Fasching

Assistant Professor, University of South Florida

Darrell Fasching was Assistant Dean of Hendricks Memorial Chapel at Syracuse University from 1975 to 1980. It was during this period that he organized the symposium on which this book is based. He received his B. A. in Philosophy from the University of Minnesota (1968) and his M.A. (1972) and Ph.D. (1978) from the Department of Religion at Syracuse University. His articles on ethics and technology have appeared in Soundings and the California Management Review, and his book The Thought of Jacques Ellul, (New York and Toronto: Edwin Mellen Press, 1981) dealt with that theologian's ethics for a technological civilization. Dr. Fasching taught at Le Moyne College in Syracuse N. Y. from 1980 to 1982 and has been Assistant Professor of Religious Studies at the University of South Florida, Tampa, since 1982. His sermon, "The Church, The Synagogue and the Gospel," won a 1980 sermon award from the National Institute for Campus Ministry and was published in the Fall 1980 NICM Journal.

Dr. Eugene Fisher

Executive Director, Office of Catholic-Jewish Relations, National Conference of Catholic Bishops

Eugene Fisher is Adjunct Professor of Hebrew Scriptures at the University of Detroit and the first lay person to hold the N.C.C.B. post. He has served on the Planning Committee for the Third National Workshop on Christian-Jewish Relations. He holds a B.A. from Sacred Heart Seminary in Detroit, an M.A. in Catholic Theology from the University of Detroit, an M.A. and Ph.D. in Hebrew Studies from N.Y.U. He is the author of numerous articles and the book, Faith Without Prejudice, Rebuilding Christian Attitudes Toward Judaism, NY: Paulist Press, 1977, and the Formation of Social Policy in the Catholic and Jewish Traditions, Notre Dame University Press, 1980, co-authored with Rabbi Daniel Polish.

Dr. Samuel Sandmel

Samuel Sandmel was author of some twenty books, most dealing directly or indirectly with Jewish-Christian issues and concerns. Among them; A Jewish Understanding of the New Testament, KTAV, 1956; We Jews and Jesus, Oxford University Press, 1965; We Jews and You Christians, J. B. Lippincott Co., 1967 and Anti-Semitism in the New Testament?, Fortress Press, 1978. Dr. Sandmel received his B. A. from the University of Missouri in 1932 and his Ph.D. from Yale in 1949 where he also directed the Hillel foundation from 1946 to 1949. He was Hillel Professor of Jewish Literature and Thought at Vanderbilt University from 1940-1952 and Professor of Bible and Hellenistic Literature at Hebrew Union College, Cincinnati, from 1952 until his retirement in 1979. During these twenty six years he served as Provost from 1957 to 1966, as editor of the Hebrew Union College Annual from 1970 to 1973 and as Director of Graduate Studies from 1973 to 1977. He was also named Distinguished Service Professor in 1966. Upon his retirement if 1979, he was accorded the rank of Professor Emeritus by Hebrew Union College. He then accepted an appointment as Hellen A. Regenstein Professor of Religion at the University of Chicago Divinity School. Samuel Sandmel was the recipient of several honorary degrees during his career as well as visiting professor and/or lecturer at numerous American and European universities. He died at age 68 on November 4, 1979, survived by his wife and three sons.

Dr. Krister Stendahl

Professor, Harvard Divinity School

Krister Stendahl, a distinguished New Testament scholar, served as Dean of Harvard Divinity School from 1968 to 1979, where he now teaches Preaching and Worship, as well as New Testament. He is the author of numerous articles and books in the area of New Testament studies, including his most recent work, Paul Among Jews and Gentiles, Philadelphia: Fortress Press, 1976. He is Moderator of the Consultation on the Church and the Jewish People for the World Council of Churches, and is a member of the World Union of Jewish Studies. He has studied in Cambridge (England) and Paris, and received his Th.D. degree from Uppsala University.

SYMPOSIUM SERIES

1. Jurgen Moltman *et al.*, **Religion and Political Society**

2. James Grace, editor, **God, Sex, and the Social Project: The Glassboro Papers on Religion and Human Sexuality**

3. M. Darrol Bryant and Herbert Richardson, editors, **A Time for Consideration: A Scholarly Appraisal of the Unification Church**

4. Donald G. Jones, editor, **Private and Public Ethics: Tensions Between Conscience and Institutional Responsibility**

5. Herbert Richardson, editor, **New Religions and Mental Health: Understanding the Issues**

6. Sheila Greeve Davaney, editor, **Feminism and Process Thought: The Harvard Divinity School/Claremont Center for Process Studies Symposium Papers**

7. International Movement, A.T.D./Fourth World, **Children of Our Time: The Children of the Fourth World**

8. Jenny Hammett, **Woman's Transformations: A Psychological Theology**

9. S. Daniel Breslauer, **A New Jewish Ethics**

10. Darrell J. Fasching, editor, **The Jewish People in Christian Preaching**

11. Henry Vander Goot, **Interpreting the Bible in Theology and the Church**

12. Everett Ferguson, **Demonology of the Early Christian World**